other books by Elyse Sommer

Decoupage Old and New
Rock and Stone Craft
Contemporary Costume Jewelry
The Bread Dough Craft Book
Designing with Cutouts
Make It with Burlap
Inventive Fiber Crafts
Career Opportunities in Crafts

WITH MIKE SOMMER

Creating with Driftwood and Weathered Wood
A New Look at Crochet
A New Look at Felt
Wearable Crafts
A New Look at Knitting

WITH JOELLEN SOMMER

Sew Your Own Accessories
A Patchwork, Appliqué and Quilting Primer

WITH RENIE BRESKIN ADAMS

Pillowmaking as Art and Craft

Textile Collector's Guide

VALUABLES . . . USABLES . . . REUSABLES

by Elyse Sommer

PHOTOGRAPHS BY MIKE SOMMER

Monarch

COPYRIGHT © 1978 BY ELYSE SOMMER
ALL RIGHTS RESERVED
INCLUDING THE RIGHT OF REPRODUCTION
IN WHOLE OR IN PART IN ANY FORM
PUBLISHED BY MONARCH
A SIMON & SCHUSTER DIVISION OF
GULF & WESTERN CORPORATION
SIMON & SCHUSTER BUILDING
1230 AVENUE OF THE AMERICAS
NEW YORK, NEW YORK 10020

DESIGNED BY IRVING PERKINS
MANUFACTURED IN THE UNITED STATES OF AMERICA
1   2   3   4   5   6   7   8   9   10

LIBRARY OF CONGRESS CATALOGING IN PUBLICATION DATA
Sommer, Elyse.
   Textile Collector's Guide
   1. Textile fabrics—Collectors and collecting.
I.   Title.
TS1306.A1S65   677'.02864'075   77-17103
ISBN 0-671-18093-2

Contents

Preface

This book is for people who love fibers and fabrics—to look at, to touch, and to use. It is for people who are creative—creative in their appreciation of hand-wrought and embellished cloth; creative in their ability to see new uses for the things created to serve outmoded functions; creative in using their own skills, if need be, not only to rescue old and unwanted treasures from obscurity and deterioration, but to give them a new life in our contemporary world. This book does not purport to be a definitive textile treatise. Its intent is to present the many possibilities for pleasure which a wide-open approach to textiles affords. The Annotated Resource Guide which concludes this volume provides the reader with the key toward in-depth pursuits of particular topics.

While my name appears on the cover, everything within these pages is the result of the generosity of people in all areas of textile endeavors. From private collectors to curators and conservators, everyone whose help I enlisted shared their knowledge, their treasures and, when Mike's camera was too far away, their own photographs. I've tried to thank everyone by bringing my own best efforts to the overall project.

There is yet another group, a vast army of unknowns, to whom all of us owe a huge debt of gratitude, and it is in deference to them that I have used the female pronoun as a predominant form of gender reference, contrary to usual publishing practice. Far from making this a for-women-only book, this is simply a small but meaningful tribute to the incredible patience and artistry of the women who have stitched and woven the bulk of the fabric and fiber objects which document the history of textiles and the evolution of taste.

ELYSE SOMMER

Woodmere, New York

ACKNOWLEDGMENTS

For their help in providing information, objects for photography, and actual photographs, I wish to thank the following people:

John D. Block, Tara Ana Finley, and Mee-Seen Loong of PB Eighty-Four; Rachel Maines, Center for the History of American Needlework; Irene Preston Miller, the Niddy Noddy; Karen Strum; presiding supervisor, Town of Hempstead, Francis T. Purcell, and Ruth Brucia, curator, Rock Hall Museum; Bucky and W. Staunton King; Merry Bean; Joan Schulze; Marcia and Ron Spark; Elizabeth Gurrier; Otto Charles Thieme; Mardel Esping; Mary E. Stinger; Carolanne Rossin, Rosycheeks; Larry Edman; Sally Kinsey, Bruce Havens, Michael Bogle of Syracuse University; Susanna E. Lewis; June and Stanford Erickson; Margaret and Bradley Brown; Eleanor and John Dimoff; Amy Solomon; Judy Dodds; Diana Willner; B. J. Adams; Norma Papish; Lynne Parker, Pot Pourri Antiques; Nancy and Dewey Lipe; Marilyn Green; John Stimpson; Sharon La Pierre; Dee Weber; William W. Robinson, South Carolina Arts Commission; Mona Costa; Liese Bronfenbrenner; Kay Ritter; Incorporated Gallery; Kari Lonning; Dan Storper, Putumayo Gallery; Lewis Smith; Paula, Dan, and Jennifer Simon; Jane Gehring; Steven Blumrich; Cathy Parenti; Sedig Malikyar; Yvonne Porcella; Phalice Ayers; Roz Belford; Norma Minkowitz; Margaret M. Hanson; and a very special thanks to Madelyn Larsen, collector-editor par excellence.

Textile Collector's Guide

1.
Welcome to the Wonderful World of Textile Collectibles

What Are Textile Collectibles?

To some the words evoke visions of ancient tapestries, costly Oriental carpets, delicate fragments from long-lost cultures—in short, the stuff which would throw a textile curator into a state of frenzied delight. Indeed, all these things are part of the world of textiles, but only part.

Textile collectibles encompass the bed, floor, and table coverings stitched, looped, woven, and hooked by our grandmothers and great-grandmothers and their great-grandmothers, first out of necessity and later as a form of creative self-expression.

Textile collectibles don't even have to be handmade if the eagerness with which certain commercially made fiber and fabric items are today being sought out by people of all ages. As for antiquity—while a really old sampler or embroidered ecclesiastic garment is indeed to be treasured, "collectible" is *not* necessarily tantamount to "antique." Thus, if your interests do not lie in the past, you can nevertheless indulge your liking for the color and softness and warmth of textiles by collecting from the present, which, thanks to the enormous interest in relearning and reinterpreting the techniques of the past, may well come to be known as the golden renaissance of textiles.

Finally, since most people who love fibers and fabrics are interested in the processes by which they are wrought, it is only natural to collect not only the end products of the loom, the crochet hook, knitting needle, and bobbin, but the tools themselves. This expansion of the concept of textiles to include things which are in turn textile-related

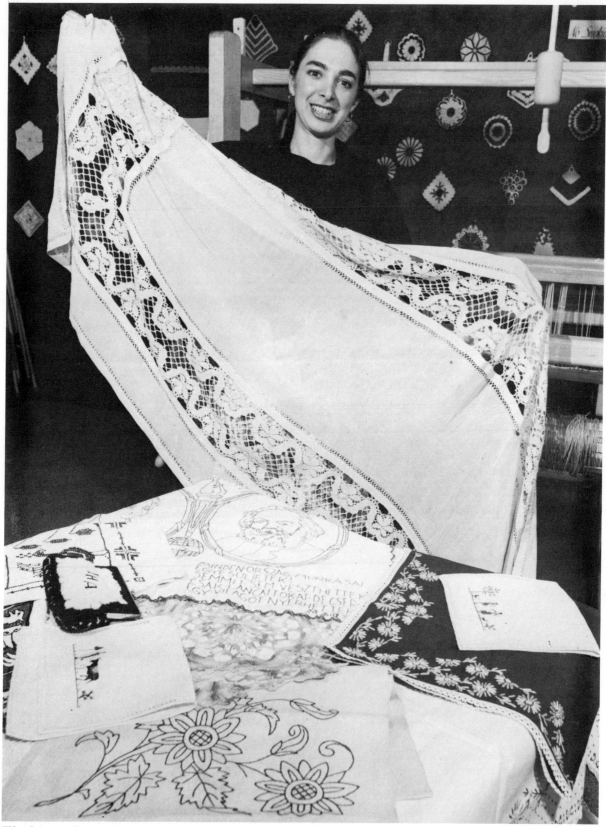

The household textiles used and made by our grandmothers and great-grandmothers and their great-grandmothers represent another important facet of the story of textiles. The Center for the History of American Needlework is an organization especially created to uphold this heritage for present and future generations. In this photograph we see the Center's dedicated director, Rachel Maines, with some of C.H.A.N.'s holdings. Photo Newman-Schmidt.

The textile enthusiast is often as interested in the materials and tools used to fashion the fabric as in the end product, and a primitive Indian loom like this would be a treasured collectible. Photographed at the Niddy Noddy, Croton-on-Hudson, New York.

opens the door to those, like myself, with a penchant for paper memorabilia—books and magazines giving history and background and how-to information about textiles to collect and to make.

On Becoming a Collector

Aside from the fact that there seems to be something of interest for every taste, talent, and age under the catchall umbrella of textiles, there's the fact that good things are still available and, what's more, available at prices to fit every budget. Collecting can and often does begin in your own or some relative's storage trunks or closets, or it can take you as far afield as a jumbo jet will carry you. It can be eclectic and casual, a matter of saving rather than throwing away, or intense and highly selective.

As with anything in life, what you learn in the process of collecting depends upon you. You can simply choose and use your accumulated treasures for their visual and tactile appeal. Old things, especially those inherited from or given by someone connected with you or your family, provide emotional as well as physical pleasure. If you're interested in how things are made and why and where, your collecting can bring with it a feast of knowledge which will in turn help you to collect more wisely. The more you know, the more involved you will become and it is no small coincidence that so many textile collectors are also actively engaged as fiber artists, lecturers, or teachers, vocationally as well as avocationally.

Defining Availability and Affordability

Once you start collecting you're bound to run into some old-time textile buffs who will regale you with tales about all the things which are "gone" (probably because they themselves were lucky enough to squirrel them away) and that people were practically giving away just a few years ago.

The reality of all collecting is that there will always be some things which are snapped up by early bird collectors or by museums. However, even the "all gone" things have a way of becoming available again as a result of the inevitabilities of death, economics, changing lifestyles, and interests. Furthermore, if a general category has sufficient inherent scope, something will always appear within the creative collector's range of vision and give rise to a new type of collectible. The very existence of this book is proof that textiles do indeed have this scope.

Finally, certain shortages add excitement to the chase. The serious collector will be challenged to track down the best of the "star" items. The tight-budget collector will find added stimulation in ferreting out valuables-in-the-making and inventing ways to enjoy and use the less than perfect. The possibilities for this type of collecting, while already discovered by many, are far from exhausted.

Even in the area of usable and reusable items you will find old-timers ready to tell you how even the junk for which you now pay dollars once cost only pennies, but then whoever said inflation stopped at the supermarket checkout counter? The most dedicated old-time

Small bits of lace and other textiles can be enjoyed even if not inherently valuable. The trick is to invent new uses and display backgrounds—like this lace fabric "displayed" on a handmade fabric bag by Karin Strum.

textile enthusiasts I've met are continuing to buy the new as well as the old. Common sense and an enterprising spirit are your best bet for avoiding what I call collector's masochism, the habit of constantly comparing today's price tags with those of yesterday. If you compare the price of what you buy with what you would have to pay for similar goods and services—i.e., a commercial bedspread compared to a large antique shawl which could serve the same purpose, or a new dress compared to a wonderful old costume, or a hanging made by a living artist compared to a mass-produced ornament—you will find that textile collectibles offer much in the way of uniqueness, quality, and value. The price you pay today is almost certain to go up next year or the year after, though it is unlikely that you will be able to retire on the proceeds. Geraldine Schneider, whose humorous comments on collecting often appear in the *New York State Antiques Almanac*, offers the following bit of whimsy to new collectors unable to match the old-timers' bargains:

A COLLECTOR'S LAMENT

My friends know I'm a Collector
They come to see each find,
However, their reaction . . .
Is enough to blow my mind.

I say "See my hanging tapestry,
My hooked colonial rug
My alphabet needlepoint sampler
(With the charming reversed letter.)"

"Mm, hm, very nice," they say, "but
My Grandmother threw out better."

"See my damask pillow slips,
My crocheted antimacassar
My homespun candlewick bedspread
(The stitch is called Prince's Feather)."

Still that familiar old refrain,
"My Grandmother threw out better."

I'm sure your Grandma's very nice
And though I've never met her,
No matter what treasures I find,
She surely threw out better!

2.
Finding Your Way Along the Textile Trail

The trail traveled by the textile enthusiast is dotted with all kinds of shops and galleries, indoor and outdoor markets, and auction houses. For the collector on a shoestring budget, the more expensive antique shops and auction houses will be primarily educational browsing stops to arm oneself with the know-how needed to spot those once-in-awhile super buys, and to indulge in an occasional splurge. The more affluent collector is likely to concentrate on these places. However, no one is ever too rich not to be thrilled by the potential of uncovering a jewel in the junk heap, so that all collectors may and indeed do converge upon the entire trail. Following are the most likely stops for good and interesting buys.

Other People's Garages, Yards, and Basements

If you're lucky, someone in your family was a saver so that even if some nimble-fingered kinswoman's patiently and prodigiously produced and accumulated textiles are no longer considered stylish or useful, they were stowed away into empty trunks and drawers. If everyone in your family is from the toss-it-out school, your best bet is to look for others who just happen to be in the process of making room or dissolving their households. At one time spring was the best time to look for these events and indeed announcements of tag, moving, garage, or yard sales seem to blossom in full force along with the crocuses. However, as more people seem to be both on the move and in need of thinning out their belongings, even more are accumu-

*Textile Collector's
Guide*

The textile collector will find
interesting things all over.
After seeing this example of
needlepoint on perforated paper
in the entry hall of Rock
Hall, a Long Island Historical
preservation, we saw several
similar ones within a five-mile
radius.

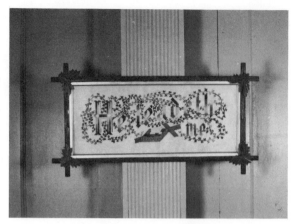

*Here's another perforated paper needlepoint at a garage sale, along with quilts and coverlets of varying ages
and quality, several souvenir pincushions, baskets, and basketry lampshades. The paisley shawl was not
quite in the same league with Madelyn Larsen's auction-bought example which you will see a bit further on.*

lating, and this combination has made the at-home sale a year-round thing. For some, it's a whole way of life. Numerous people, mostly women who once shopped the garage sales themselves, have become tag sale specialists, helping others to price, set up, and advertise their sales for a percentage of the "take." One elderly woman I know spends several days each week going out to distant neighborhoods, buying things, then holding weekend yard sales with her new purchases. She may not be getting rich from this kind of wheeling and dealing, but she has a constant flow of visitors to her home and has in the process acquired a male friend who now takes her "picking." On the whole, yard sales represent occasional housecleaning-for-profit events for individual homeowners.

The chances of finding a rare textile treasure are considerably better than winning a huge prize in a lottery, but it's an outside chance nevertheless, and it takes shoe leather, gasoline, and perseverance to work your way through enough sales to unearth some great buys. If you live in a fairly big city you can keep busy for the better part of each weekend wandering from garage to yard to basement within your particular neighborhood. This kind of local collecting is a good chance for combining buying with exercise. I use my bike for local or near-local garage sales. My basket holds all kinds of small goodies and I'm delighted to come back for anything bigger.

To find out about local sales, watch the bulletin boards at the entrances and exits of food stores, posted signs on trees, telephone poles, and ads in the local Pennysavers and weekly newspapers. For a larger geographic range, go through the household sale ads in the metropolitan papers.

To refine your list of stops, look for ads which itemize what is being offered and pick out those which refer to fiber and fabric items. If a phone number is given, call first and ask if there are any linens, quilts, rugs, or other items of this type. Look for multifamily sales where neighbors consolidate their publicity and advertising efforts. Professional tag sales tend to carry higher price tags but they often have more and better things. Some tag sale organizers will notify you of special-interest sales.

Go early, the way dealers do. Either call and explain that you can't come or just take a chance and walk in. People may not be as ready to bargain, but by the same token they are still fresh and eager, anxious to make their first sale for "good luck" during the rest of the sale. Most importantly, it's your chance to have the first opportunity to see and buy anything unusual. If there's something special you want, ask. Sometimes people don't put things out because they forget or because they didn't think anyone would be interested.

Flea Markets

In the West they are called swap meets. By any name they are basically giant garage sales. Instead of going to an individual's house, you go to a single marketplace where sellers rent space in order to display their wares for the day. In the twenty or so years that flea markets have become part of the American scene, they have expanded enormously. Not only do private householders join in, but dealers of every kind of new and second-hand merchandise set up shop weekend after weekend, always renting the same space. Like garage sales, flea markets reach their peak from spring through summer, but due to their soaring popularity many keep going all year long, moving from parking lots and other outdoor sites to indoor locations.

For the textile collector, more does not necessarily mean better since many of the more honky-tonk markets have attracted the kind of vendors who drive out the more interesting ones. Nevertheless, flea markets are here to stay and patience and fortitude will continue to bring rewards. I recently went to a Sunday flea market at a local mall parking lot. The smell of hot dogs and the crush of shoddy junk almost made me forfeit my drive-in fee and turn around. However, the habit of looking everywhere "just in case" is too ingrained and so I worked my way from row to row. I discovered a lady who, to keep her husband company while he sold job-lot sweatshirts, had brought along her own vast collection of old household lace goods. I also found a beaded Victorian pincushion thrown in a box of doll clothes by a doll specialist, one she was happy to be rid of for a couple of dollars, and an old embroidery instruction booklet for fifty cents. One never knows!

The best time to go to a flea market is very early—when the dealers are first setting up and are in fact busy trading with one another. Years ago, before the Flea Market in Englishtown, New Jersey, was still undiscovered by the popular press, we used to leave our Long Island home before dawn and arrive at the market before sunup. By the time we'd finished going through the aisles, bundled up in warm clothes to ward off the early morning chill, it felt like lunch when we breakfasted on tantalizing ham sandwiches and hot coffee bought from the farm food stands.

Shops

Whether you're looking for bargains, rarities, old, or contemporary collectibles, there's a store for everything. *Thrift shops,* run by churches and other charitable organizations, are favorites with bargain hunters, though stories about rare tapestries bought at incredibly low prices have gotten around sufficiently to have made managers of thrift shops careful about evaluating their donated goods, even if they have to hire appraisers. Stories have in turn circulated about special customers or collecting organizations being "tipped off." Fortunately, most if not all textiles are still considered oddments not worth bothering with so that thrift-shop bargains are not a thing of the past.

Telling the manager that you are actually looking for certain kinds of materials or needlework or old bags, scarves, or hankies is not going to send prices soaring. In fact, if the thrift shop is in the neighborhood and you stop in regularly the manager may well think of you as the hankie or tablecloth customer and put things aside for you. This does not mean of course that you should go about bragging about how much you think some of these things are worth or the fabulous things you will do to make them valuable.

Telling the person running an *antique shop* that you are interested in particular items once again is not tantamount to being "taken." Shop owners are much more interested in and likely to be helpful to potential buyers than just lookers. So-called posh antique dealers often have less-than-choice collectibles in their back rooms so if you're a budget collector or a dedicated recycler, ask if there are any less-than-perfect things around. The dealer may be happy to sell them if he or she has them, and be more inclined to chat with you and provide interesting bits of general information once you are a customer, no matter how modest.

Not all antique shops are exclusive or stocked with expensive valuables, and the many derivatives such as Junktiques and Interestiques are crosses between antique and thrift shops, under private ownership. Location also affects the nature of the shop, with anyplace in a resort

Thrift-shop buys are often as good as your ingenuity for recycling them into something new. This dainty blouse is the end product of a hand-crocheted tablecloth bought in imperfect condition. The motifs were cut apart and edged with cotton thread, using crochet and knotless netting or buttonhole stitches. The necklace was salvaged from an old needlepoint bag with a broken handle and several holes.

area being higher since there are higher rents to absorb. However, resorts with off seasons may also have off-season prices so *when* you travel the textile trail is likely to affect what you find and what you will pay for it.

The outpouring of creative energy on the part of contemporary artists and craftspersons has been accompanied by the opening of many fine *contemporary crafts gallery shops,* most of which carry some textiles; some may specialize in them. *Supply shops* carrying fine yarns and fiber tools often have galleries for the sale of both domestic and quality imported textiles. Many artists sell directly from their studios and information about where to find these outlets may be found in Chapter 8, Annotated Resource Guide.

Shows

The difference between a flea market and a show or fair is that the former is a conglomeration of old and new, good and bad; while the show or fair, at least if it's a good one, represents the best that the seller has to offer. In the case of the most prestigious and exclusive, sellers are present by invitation only. Crafts fairs have become as ubiquitous as antique shows and just as the poor-quality antique shows are more "flea" than antique so the poorer crafts show tends to resemble a church bazaar. A good show in either category will offer the collector a fast and enjoyable way to obtain an overview of the best things being offered, and the going prices. The most worthwhile are those which are regularly scheduled events, with established reputations. Antique and crafts magazines (see Chapter 8) not only list announcements of various shows, but often carry reviews.

There are also combination antique-crafts shows and while the kinship is a solid one, the majority of these combination affairs lack the quality of the specialized ones. When you visit any show, talk to the dealers. Keep in mind that their displays are limited to what their trucks and campers will hold and their booths accommodate, usually the cream of their crop. The fair is your chance not only to window- or booth-shop or buy, but to make contacts for visits to home shops. Years ago I was looking for two matching spool chests as end tables for my living room. When I visited the prestigious New York Madison Square Garden antiques show, I looked in each booth, to no avail. Whenever I saw a dealer who was located within a reasonable driving distance from my home I inquired about spool chests. One dealer who was a pine specialist told me that indeed he did have a number of chests in his barn. That barn also yielded two still-used chests (see page 103) as well as numerous other goodies such as a log cabin quilt and some nice lace items.

"Going, going . . . sold!" There's a certain magic to the jargon of the auctioneer and the atmosphere of the auction, whether held on the lawn of an old house, in the barn of a farm, or in the high-ceilinged rooms of a large auction house. For the textile collector a country auction might yield an old spinning wheel, a box of old needle-work, or household linens. Often the best buys are part of odd lots, not considered worth special itemization. A cursory look at ads of the big-city auction houses would indicate that Oriental carpets are the primary textile drawing cards, since these are listed most frequently. However, once you start watching ads such as the Friday auction list-ings in *The New York Times* you will notice among the nontextile things such items as Kashmir shawls, a seventeenth-century stump-work box or picture, tapestries, ecclesiastical items, and domestic and folk art fabrics. Some of the latter are even considered important enough for special sales and I was not at all surprised when John Block, the director of Sotheby Parke Bernet's budget annex, PB Eighty-Four, cited Persian, Egyptian, and Islamic textiles as good

Some auctions will be especially geared to textiles, but lots of good and interesting buys can be found at general household sales. Rugs are almost always in evidence, as at this PB Eighty-Four auction preview, but I've also seen quilts, small tapestries, and embroideries at similar "general" auctions.

investment prospects. He considers Peruvian items the best bet for beginners. While the big auction sales are not likely to be in the thrift-shop price league, neither is everything astronomically high.

Madelyn Larsen bought her genuine pieced Kashmir shawl at a Manhattan auction for $30 ten years ago. Today, with the increase of interest in all manner of patchwork, I've seen auction catalogues estimate values at $200 and up, though this does not necessarily mean that the estimated price will be the final one. What's more, there's always some new and as yet uninflated item to consider. At a more recent auction, also in Manhattan, two Chancay fragments circa A.D. 1000–1400, one mounted and one with two bands of stylized figures, sold at $30 and $40, though the gallery's estimates had been considerably higher. Two square medallions with goat figures made for Al-Mukhtadi in the late 7th-8th century sold for $90, a price PB Eighty-Four's textile expert, Tara Ana Finley, considered a true bargain. The same sale contained items which did sell in the thousands, and auctioneers in other cities could cite similar ranges along the price scale.

Whether you plan to buy something for $5 or $5000 *never, never* bid unless you have first gone to the auction preview. Without a careful inspection of the back as well as the front of her Kashmir

No matter what type of auction you attend, be sure to be there during the preview inspection. Without this type of inspection of the back as well as front, Madelyn Larsen could not have seen the piecing of the embroidered woven parts which made up her Kashmir shawl—or for that matter spotted the date, 1830 in our numbering system, woven into the border.

Madelyn uses her shawl as a bedcover, with a larger backing of black cotton. We enjoyed borrowing it for our dining-room table.

shawl, Madelyn Larsen would not have been able to establish its pieced construction, nor would she have had a chance to spot the date, 1830, woven into one corner of the border. In addition to checking provenance and quality, the textile buyer can check to see if a fabric is glued to a board, something which can be hard to undo.

For those readers collecting primarily items made in the present, opportunities for buying at auction are more limited but by no means nonexistent. The weavers of the Crown Point Rug Weavers' Association in New Mexico, for example, sell their rugs at regularly scheduled auction sales to which people travel from all over the country (see Chapter 4, Navajo Rugs, and Chapter 8, Organizations). Crafts organizations find auctions a pleasant and successful way to raise funds. The Long Island Craftsmen's Guild holds an annual auction which has become an established annual event.

3.
Anatomy of an All-Encompassing Collection of Valuables, Usables, and Reusables

Once you become involved in old textiles you won't have to go far to find other people who share your enthusiasm. You *may* have to go far before you encounter a collector as experienced, knowledgeable, and truly diversified as Bucky King. Her collection and collecting methods and advice embody the overall approach of this book. Future chapters and examples from other textile enthusiasts' collections will confirm and elaborate upon Bucky's astute recommendations and predictions.

Like many textile people Bucky is the granddaughter of an accomplished needlewoman. She recalls being bitten by the fiber-collecting bug somewhere around the age of twelve or fourteen, when her grandmother presented her with an antique sewing kit, complete with tiny scissors. Her early collecting was reinforced by the entire family's habit of saving any well-executed handmade piece which might one day be used again. It is this ingrained respect for the old techniques and the time and patience involved in their creation, combined with their charm and personality, that comprises the motivation for Bucky's collecting. As she puts it, "There's something of the person who made it in each piece."

The King collection spans more than two decades of buying forays to auctions, estate sales, and thrift shops. It also includes bequests from relatives and friends who knew Bucky would give their treasures

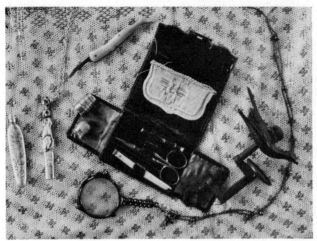

A sewing kit launched Bucky King's extensive textile collection. The pictured example is German, circa 1874. To the right of the case, a German-made sewing bird with a tiny pincushion mounted on the bird's back, circa 1880. At the top left is a knife for cutting thread, its carved ivory handle in the shape of a lady's leg. Since Bucky uses this constantly for her tapestry weavings her students often accuse her of using "her old leg to cut with." On the far left are two beautiful French sterling silver needle cases, circa 1871. An antique magnifying glass reveals a detail of an Egyptian shawl worked in hand netting and embossed with 10-carat gold section plates, circa 1887–1890.

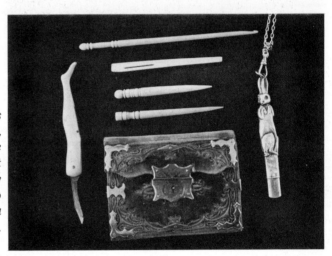

The exterior view of the needlecase reveals metal-trimmed rose velvet. To the left of the case, a better view of the ivory leg threadcutter. The closeup view of the needle holder at the right reveals its shape to be that of a rabbit, with ruby eye and a removable tail. At the top of the photo we see four ivory tools: a crochet hook, a weaving needle, and two punches.

a loving home. Its growth has been accompanied by a satisfying career as co-owner in a supply and teaching studio and as an accomplished fiber crafts artist. Here are just some of the fiber techniques and tools Bucky King has accumulated:

· Antique quilts and coverlets
· Clothing and accessories, ranging from a perfect nineteenth century mandarin coat to collars and bags
· Needlework kits and tools, as well as those used for spinning and weaving
· Weaving, embroidery, and lace samples
· A "mess of oddments," exclusive of household linen of which Bucky is not particularly fond but which she does keep as a separate collection since her extensive buying, especially at estate sales, has led her to many valuables too good to pass up
· Contemporary fiber crafts

*An All-Encompassing
Collection*

Just as Bucky King generously shares bits and pieces of her collection with students, she patiently answered my questions about how, why, and where she collects, with a view toward providing the reader with a basis for starting out as a collector. Here then are the highlights of our interview:

E.S.: Did you ever consider specializing in any particular area of fibers?
B.K.: I have never tried to specialize in any one area because I always felt it was wiser to have a general collection of as many diversified methods and tools as possible.
E.S.: If you did not specialize by category, did you have any restrictions on your collecting in terms of money expenditures?

Bucky King's clothing collection includes this beautifully embroidered Chinese mandarin silk coat. It was brought to the United States by Admiral Sidney Staunton around 1870, after Pres. Fillmore had dispatched the naval fleet to China as a gesture of goodwill.

B.K.: I have always bought according to what I can afford and that range is geared to between $25 and $100, with a great percentage of purchases being under $10. While I put a dollar limit on my spending, I was always happily willing to read and study up on everything. Knowing about a technique or tool, being able to tell if something is valuable or not, or worthy of collecting has stood me well at auctions, flea markets, and country sales. I would urge any potential collector to study the field thoroughly before plunging into it—especially if you want your collection to accrue in value over the years.

E.S.: Does your affordability yardstick apply to today's all-around inflationary price picture?

B.K.: While Wyoming where I live has a superb climate (clean air and water, low humidity) for the preservation of all textiles, the addiction of the average American for permanent-press fabrics, easy-care everything, has caused the price of many antique fabric items to plunge, at least here in the West. We have very few textile collectors, though vast supplies are stored lovingly in attics for fifty years or more and many of these can still be bought at country auctions. It is not uncommon to buy a whole bag of beautifully crocheted oddments for $1 and $3. (Author's Note: The old adage about going West most assuredly applies since that price range tends to apply to each *piece* within a box in the East!)

E.S.: Do you feel the *under* $25 buys are limited to what you call oddments nowadays?

For the imaginative collector, handmade household items are fruitful beginnings for wearable contemporary clothing, like this handsome jacket made from a bedspread knitted circa 1925–1930. The cut sections were overcast on a sewing machine, with crochet trim added down the front and on the sleeves. The nonhandy collector would have to add the cost of an artisan's labor to the initial purchase.

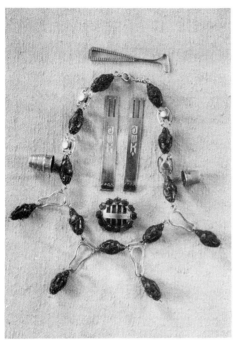

For the antique clothing collector the nonfiber parts can be the most valuable. As a case in point, Bucky's necklace was made from solid gold Tiffany garters which had been attached to her aunt Mary Lynn's wedding corset (1918). The rosewood beads, each carved with a different Chinese figure, were a $2 thrift-shop find. Other items of interest in this picture: Grandmother's first child thimble from the 1870s, Bucky's 112-year-old gold thimble, an 18-carat gold Tiffany shoebutton hook (top of the necklace), a pair of men's solid gold evening garters with slots and son John David Millard King's initials. Underneath the garters is a Victorian gold pin with real hair woven into the tiny circles.

As you will see as you continue through this book, there's a bag for every textile technique and era. Here are three small beaded bags. The tiny steel jet and crocheted bag is the oldest of the three. The pouch at right features strip beading done extensively in the 1920s, and the envelope bag is individually beaded in brown, rust, green, and red beads, with a silk cord handle, circa 1922.

B.K.: Not if you have vision and patience. Last year I waited two hours at a country auction for a small trunk of antique baby clothes and crochet pieces to be brought out. It began to snow and as more people left, the auctioneer began to put up several items together. Finally the little old trunk came up, along with three hideous old moth-eaten blankets, a stack of old records, ten old books and two used gas cans. I paid $15 for the lot and was embarrassed to carry off the rest of the junk but felt obligated to at least remove it.

That trunk contained two really fine treasures—an old never-used coverlet and handspun linen thread with a date and name tag attached to it—as well as many other less valuable goodies. The old blankets I salvaged for

*Each silver and jet bead woven
to create this art nouveau
pattern is equal in size to a
pinhead. The handle and chain
are sterling silver and when it
was first offered for sale in
France, around 1910–1920, it
cost $40.*

*Here once again we see
nonclothing become a
contemporary usable/
collectible. Each bag has
its origin in a circa 1900
crochet antimacassar and is
lined with fabric and
interfacing.*

horse blankets (Bucky lives on a working ranch) and my husband, who knows something about old records, found seven in the "junk" which netted a profit of over $100. What's more, the old gas cans are very handy in my greenhouse.

As for vision, what I mean by this is the ability to see an item not just as an interesting piece in itself but also for what could be done with it. Last year, for example, I bought a handsome antique knitted bedspread for $3. This probably took someone at least a year to make and was still in fair condition. By removing the badly worn areas, about two yards, I was able to make a handsome jacket with the remaining pieces. (Author's Note: Again, go West if you want to match that $3 price, but the East does have these collectibles, too. I saw a spread very similar to the one from

The interest in laces to use, reuse, and study for their techniques is growing, growing, growing. Of course, Bucky King was way ahead of the crowd. Here we see a bobbin lace mat, circa 1910, with an authentic hand-blown lacemaker's glass lamp dating to about 1850. The bowl on top contained the oil to be burned and a tin reflector was used behind the lamp to produce a stronger light.

which Bucky made her jacket. The asking price was $8, still a good buy, and with a bit of bargaining it was secured for $6, just twice the Wyoming price.)

E.S.: Speaking of cutting up old things, how do you have the heart to cut into an old piece?

B.K.: First, it must *never* be a piece that is in good condition throughout, or museum quality so to speak. It must be worn, torn, and in bad condition. Then it is like a doctor doing a cornea transplant. There are parts that still work and can be used by someone else, so I just go ahead and cut out the good and rework it. The unusables I burn. Odd scraps are used for bags or to decorate something else. To prevent unraveling for crocheted and knitted fabrics, I bind them off on a sewing machine.

E.S.: What would you say was *the* coup of your collecting career?

B.K.: When I was still co-owner of the "Fringe and Frame" in Pittsburgh, the old Allegheny Company workhouse was about to be torn down. An auction was held to dispose of the two-harness rug looms installed there in 1916. The huge six-foot-square looms came with heavy beaters with the marks of all the former prisoners—some with days marked off for time, some with initials, some with names and dates. It took three men half a day to dismantle and load the looms onto the truck but my partner and I purchased them all for less than $4 apiece. We sold those looms at a nice profit and the people who now own them love and cherish them, not just because of their value but because of the tales they tell.

E.S.: Your collection is obviously a sizable one. How do you keep everything sorted, stored, and displayed?

B.K.: Many pieces are used, such as my spinning wheels and embroidery frames. Some antique pieces are framed and used as decorations in my home and studio. A special section of bits and pieces which can be

Antique embroidery frames are quite rare and valuable. This hand-turned walnut example, made in England in 1870, was given to Bucky by a family friend, Mrs. Bailey. The skein winder attached to the bottom of the frame is also a gift, from Dr. and Mrs. Solomon B. Freehof.

handled, touched, and examined is kept in an antique leather trunk and is, in effect, a teaching aid. Another section is stored in specially made aluminum boxes, between nonacid tissue paper, and aired at least once a year when I use them as comparison examples. Quilts and coverlets are used at least three or four weeks out of each year and then re-stored until used again.

E.S.: Could you comment on the collectibility of contemporary fiber work?

B.K.: Both contemporary fiber art and what I call unique one-of-a-kind boutique items come into play here. Buying from living artists does not mean that you will be getting bargains but since inflation seems inevitable it should be heartwarming to know that everything will rise in value. For the avid, serious fiber collector a few wall pieces are a must. I tend to lean toward artists with established reputations. In buying contemporary crafts work, if a piece is unique, original in design, made of quality fibers which will not distintegrate, pleasing to the eye and hand, and body (if worn), it is usually worth the money and a potential collector's item. Here, as in buying antiques, taste and fiber knowledge are invaluable.

E.S.: Are there any recommendations you would have in terms of availability and value potential?

B.K.: The most readily available items for present-day collecting are the crochet pieces from the 1920s to 1930s, table linens, hankies, quilt squares, baby clothes from the 1920s and 1930s, beaded bags (even though they're rising in price), umbrellas and early machine-made embroidery work from 1920 through 1924. The lovely old hand-done machine-embroidered clothing tags are a delight to collect, many on real silk!

4.
Collectors' Favorites

Bucky King's vast and wide-ranging collecting activities should convince anyone still in need of convincing that textiles do indeed offer plenty of rewards and pleasures. Not everyone will want to take this all-encompassing approach, so let's subdivide textile collectibles into some general categories for those whose time, space, budget, and personal preference dictate a more controlled type of collecting. Each category gives rise to yet more individualized and specific points of view. There always remain the refinements that accompany choices about how to collect in terms of value and condition.

Rather than to discuss various areas alphabetically or in any kind of judgmental order of importance, I have chosen to let the sequence be dictated by the most natural flow of accumulated information and illustrations. Some things discussed in one section would fit into another, but then the most specific collectors always take a few detours too, don't they? For in-depth study and collecting, readers are urged to take advantage of the many reference sources provided in Chapter 8.

Quilts and Coverlets

Bed coverings, whether woven or patched and quilted, have generally been treasured household furnishings, and there were devoted collectors well before the boom and bustle which has followed the crafts and folk art revival of the late 1960s. Although quilting and patchwork as well as weaving trace their origins to early and far-flung civilizations (the Kashmir shawl on p. 14 is a very distinctive type of woven and patched art fabric), the collecting furor of recent years has revolved primarily around examples from the American past.

THE PATCHWORK QUILT

Best known of all the bed coverings, most avidly sought and consequently continually appreciating in value, is the patchwork quilt. When one sees the stunning pictorial and graphic examples which have been more and more frequently exhibited in museums and other public places, one can only wonder, not only at the resourcefulness and instinctive design genius of the quilt-makers, but why it took the general public and the curatorial community so long to recognize and accept the quilt's value as art as well as its historic value. Be that as it may, today the patchwork quilt is without a doubt *the* star collectible among bed coverings, and textiles in general.

Families are digging quilts out of long-locked trunks and using and displaying them once again. If they have no place for them, there are buyers eager and willing to pay prices which have escalated steadily since the early 1970s. What's more, hobbyists as well as professional artists have taken up quilting so that after fifty years of quilt-making activity limited mostly to a scattering of rural communities, we are able to collect from a whole new era, the 1970s.

Those who consider old automatically better than new should keep an open mind. It is true that many a quilt being stitched today does not exemplify collector's quality craftsmanship or design, but then neither did all the products of our forebears. In the past year I have seen people pay exaggerated prices for old quilts of ordinary workmanship and design. Torn and worn areas are accepted as signs of an authentic old family heirloom. Modern reproductions of traditional patterns are not differentiated from innovative and distinctly contemporary interpretations of the quilter's craft. What these buyers do not realize is that there have always been two kinds of quilts: 1. The daily-use quilt, with function rather than creative design the foremost consideration. 2. The "best" quilt, made and used for special occasions. With new quilts the first category encompasses a vast production of do-it-yourself copies, while the second category contains the more inventive quilts which are part of what has become known and accepted as contemporary fiber art.

In the final analysis, it is your own emotional and esthetic response, coupled with your spending power, which will dictate your buying choices. To fortify your instincts and stretch your dollars, here are some facts and pointers for evaluating the how-when-where-why of quilts:

1. Dark spots in a quilt are indicative of unginned or unpurified cot-

ton, used less and less after the invention of the cotton gin in 1790. To look for these impurities, hold the quilt to the light.

2. Earliest quilts were pieced from scraps of hard-to-obtain imported chintzes and some domestic cottons. It was the shortage of fabric which resulted in the use of the many, many small pieces (some quilt owners have counted as many as 4,000 pieces) and it was while cotton was used as the primary quilt filler that stitches had to be tiny and close, to prevent the cotton from shifting around.

3. Before 1825 designs were European-inspired, with bottom-to-top, treelike symmetry and few borders. The all-over pieced block designs with borders predominated after 1825. Appliqués, while used for designs as early as 1750, reached their peak of quality and quantity between 1825 and 1870, after fabrics became more readily available.

4. Dyes are another age indicator, so that the more one knows about textiles, the easier it is to determine the approximate date. Indigo or natural dyes are a good sign of age. Antique lovers pounce upon greens faded to blue or yellow since green is known to have been an unstable color. Faded pastels, though certainly not new (usually from the 1920s), are known among experts as Depression quilts. These are considered less interesting and are less costly and more available. There are always exceptions and a Depression quilt with an unusual placement of design or an atypically dark background is something for the low-budget collector to seek out. Special commemoratives, like the quilts made after Lindbergh's flight, are special and valuable examples within the Depression period.

5. There are some 3,000 known patchwork patterns with innumerable variations. The uninformed buyer tends to look for the most common and familiar patterns in soft, light colors as a safe buy (i.e., the double wedding ring, grandmother's flower garden), but less common, more graphic designs are the ones collected by more sophisticated buyers. This is why the Amish quilts from Pennsylvania and parts of the Midwest have enjoyed a special boom. Kentucky quilts also have their special collectors, as do those made in Hawaii.

6. Several types of quilts once considered fads have enjoyed renewed interest as part of the general growth of interest in quilts. Most notable of these and fairly available is the Victorian crazy quilt, consisting of randomly pieced bits of silk, velvets, and prints with elaborate embroidery. The most collectible examples will feature some special touches such as a lithographed patch, or stitched fill-ins of people, animals, and labels.

   Less pictorially interesting is the yo-yo quilt from the 1920s. This consists of fabric circles drawn into flowerlike shapes with basting stitches. Neither of these specialty items is actually a quilt, but is more correctly called a decorative pieced top. This also brings up a point applicable to patchwork quilts: Many patchwork tops were put aside to be quilted at some future time and those which remain unquilted offer a chance to enjoy the patchwork designs at less cost than the quilted spreads.

7. Crib quilts made by and/or for children have become important collectors' specialties, boosted by the increased popularity of all things small or miniature. Beware, however, and inspect the crib quilt for signs of being a cut-down large quilt.

8. Condition *does* matter. While slightly faded colors give a pleasantly mellow look, worn and torn areas are something else again. If you collect quilts in order to make other things with them, then the damaged quilt is your special treasure, but it should be priced accordingly. (Marilyn Green of California does all her stitcheries on decayed old baby quilts bought in thrift shops. She actually lets them decay further before adding her own embellishments!) In the trade the imperfect quilt is known as a cutter quilt. I recently saw a beautiful old quilt with hundreds of lithographed silk squares of animals and flowers at an auction preview. Upon close inspection, I noticed that many of the little squares were badly worn. In perfect condition this quilt would have fetched a tidy sum, but "as is" its main appeal was to the recycler who might save enough for a jacket or use bits and pieces for some soft jewelry. $30 should have been the top price paid, and $25 actually bought it.

9. Contemporary quilts have become widely available since about 1969. Reproductions of traditional patterns are useful and offer all the wash-and-wear advantages of modern technology. Dacron and polyester fillings make extremely tiny stitching superfluous.

What about machine stitching? The patchwork quilt typifies the utilization of everything available and in our present world the sewing machine is an available and valid tool which the early quilters would have happily embraced. Rather than to base a value judgment on hand versus machine stitching, consider the method used: There is functional, time-saving machine stitching, and there is that which reflects an understanding and mastery of the machine as a creative tool.

From the collector's standpoint the contemporary quilt most worthy of consideration is that which makes its own unique statement in terms of design. Studying the quilts in exhibits and sales of contemporary fiber art, in museums and galleries and at well-screened crafts shows, reading reviews in journals like *Crafts Horizons, The Working Craftsman,* and *Fiber Arts* (see Chapter 8, Periodicals) will help you to distinguish between that which is merely funky and that which will stand alongside the best quilts of other eras. Prices of modern quilts are on the high side though the collector with good taste and judgment can discover new and still reasonably priced talent. Since items commemorating special events and incorporating special emblems and readily recognizable public places are considered highly collectible, the many fine quilts

This kingsized, machine-appliquéd and quilted Washington bicentennial quilt was made by Merry Bean. The 1776 section contains Mt. Vernon and the C & O Canal; the 1886 section includes the Smithsonian "Castle" on the mall; the 1976 section features the White House, the Capitol, Kennedy Center, the Washington Monument, and the subway. The colors are dark blue and white and the design and workmanship defies comments about contemporary craftsmanship.

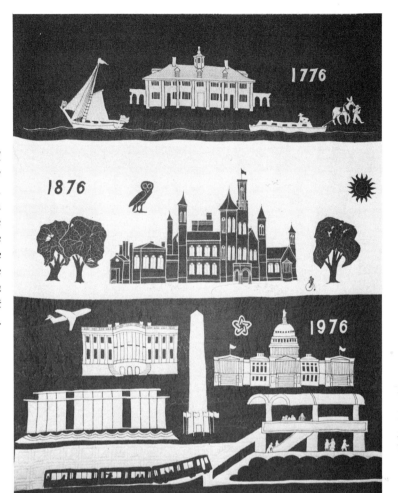

Contemporary artists like Merry Bean often sell and show their work through cooperative gallery ventures. Here we see the Washington bicentennial quilt displayed along with other fine fiber art created by members of the fiber workshop of the Torpedo Factory in Alexandria, Virginia—a good place to visit for seeing and buying this type of work.

*Joan Schulze's prizewinning bicentennial flag quilt
has an ingenious design feature: Stars centered
with little stuffed and stitched stocking faces. For
a closeup detail see page 74. Photo, Chuck Koehler.*

made for the 1976 bicentennial offers some of the outstanding
collecting opportunities today. A number of these quilts of particular interest to the antique lover were those fashioned from antique
materials especially collected by the quiltmakers. For more on this
type of collecting see pages 52–56.

COLLECTING QUILTS FOR PLEASURE AND PROFIT: A NOT ATYPICAL STORY

Sometimes you have to leave your home territory to find out about
some of its special attractions. Marcia and Ron Spark are a case in
point. Both were raised in Pennsylvania but did not become aware

of their home state's reputation for producing outstanding patchwork quilts until 1972 when Ron's medical training took them to Oak Ridge, Tennessee.

Since there wasn't much for Marcia to do, she began driving around the countryside talking to the local women and in so doing became aware of the richness which quilting brought to many of these isolated lives. She bought some of these quilts, never paying more than $15 each, since her only link to previous collecting was Ron's accumulation of 1940s ties which cost even less.

When the Sparks left Tennessee for Ron's next medical residency in Denver, Colorado, they took with them close to a dozen quilts. All were rather crude but had served to spearhead their interest in earlier and more interesting examples. Ron challenged Marcia to "do something" with what they had in order to finance more serious collecting. Not one to turn down a challenge, Marcia headed for a Denver shop, the owner of which not only took her entire "stock" but sent a dealer from Aspen, apparently desperately in need of quilts, to her house. This led to Marcia's becoming the Aspen dealer's Denver scout or "picker." The ensuing demand for her pickings (flea markets, house sales, etc.) began an intensive search for enough quilts to enable them to resell in quantity and to collect to suit their increasingly sophisticated tastes.

Ron launched the quilt search with a campaign of small ads for "pre-1940 quilts wanted." In order to go beyond the usual antique publication sources, he scoured the pages of Ayer's *Dictionary of Publications* (Author's Note: I would also recommend Ulrich's *International Periodical Directory*) for small weekly publications, especially those reaching farm families. The ads proved most productive. "The people who wrote to us were very open and honest and we were able to buy many unused quilts which had been stored away as family keepsakes," Marcia recalls. After awhile the ad responses simmered down and the Sparks then took time out to visit dealers who in turn became *their* pickers.

When Ron's career necessitated moving once again, the quilt buying and selling helped smooth the always bumpy adjustment, for their many mail-order contacts reached to their new home in Tucson, Arizona. As Marcia became more and more of a quilt scholar she gave up volume selling in order to devote most of her time to her interest in rare museum quality quilts. Since both she and Ron have a philosophy of sharing rather than hoarding, their collection is lent to museums for exhibits, and Marcia continues to wholesale even her prize quilts.

Ron's original tie collection has continued to grow too and the correlation between the two collectibles is best evidenced in Ron's marvelous tie-patchwork smoking jacket found, as if waiting for him, in an antique shop. The quilts have in turn led to other folk art interests, notably hooked rugs, some of which will be seen in the next chapter.

If the Sparks' story sounds like the stuff a collector's pipe dreams are made of, I might point out that I've come across many other collectors-turned-professional, who have traveled the same basic route, few of them involved much longer, and some for even less time. Rhea Goodman of New York started buying quilts while she was in college, spending around $35 each, and recently sold off her collection at prices ranging from $125 to $4,000! Renee Butler's quilts were bought to decorate her Potomac area home and have grown into a collection worthy of museum exhibits, also in just a few years. I saw some of them not long ago in a show at the Textile Museum in Washington, D.C., and noted a similarity in her taste and that of the Sparks. Both favor the Amish quilts, and both own unusual commemoratives of Lindbergh's flight.

Marcia and Ron Spark show some of the outstanding quilts in their collection: On the wall is a barn raising version of the popular log cabin design, circa 1880. This typifies the graphic impact which has made quilts the favorite collectibles of artists such as Andy Warhol and Kenneth Knowland. Ron holds an unusual schoolhouse quilt with individually stuffed door handles, and below is an eagle quilt made to commemorate Lindbergh's flight in 1928. Ron's jacket vividly illustrates the relationship between his tie collection and the husband-wife quilt collection. (See pages 69–70 for details.)

Patchwork and appliqué quilts have become star collectibles not only because of their appeal to a very wide range of tastes but because they were produced and preserved in much greater profusion than some of the other types of bed coverings. The all-white quilt, for example, though considered in its day (late eighteenth and early nineteenth century) more of a design challenge than patchwork, is reputed to have been limited in production by a one-time law restricting the purchase and use of scarce cotton materials. Fortunately a number of modern fabric artists have translated all- or almost all-white trapunto work into quilts well worth the serious collector's attention. Elizabeth Gurrier of Hollis, New Hampshire, and Elsa Brown of Rising Ridge, Connecticut, are outstanding practitioners.

Other types of bed coverings have made their impact on present-day lives via commercial reproductions. The candlewick spread served as the inspiration for the ubiquitous daily-use chenille spread (many of the more flamboyant of these are already attracting young collectors, especially collector-recyclers), and many traditional upholstery and curtain fabrics are copies of the printed fabrics used for "whole-cloth" spreads and bed hangings. Few intact examples of whole-cloth spreads and hangings are available to the average collector. However, good-sized fragments of the original copperplate printed fabrics have survived and make for a very attractive collection, with handsome fragments available in a $25 to $40 price range.

Knitted and crocheted bedspreads from the Victorian era and later have held up rather well and these have been enjoying a steady renaissance.

"Club Circle," a contemporary white trapunto quilt by Elizabeth Gurrier. Photo courtesy of artist

A Jacquard woven coverlet, subject of a five-year research project by its owner, Otto Thieme.

Toile de Jouy whole-cloth spreads and bed hangings are found mostly in the collections of museums and historical restorations—like this beautiful bed with its original furnishings, plus personal accessories photographed at Rock Hall in Lawrence, New York. Collectors can obtain fragments of original copperplate prints.

WOVEN COVERLETS

Woven coverlets have been sought out by many as practical antiques. They also attract a large contingent of dedicated collectors.

Probably one of the most sought after types of coverlets is the Jacquard, named after a Frenchman, Joseph Jacquard, who invented a loom which made it possible to weave elaborate patterns on wide cloths. The Jacquard loom was brought to the United States around 1820, and the coverlets made after this date frequently represent a collaboration between a professional weaver and the housewife/patron who provided handspun and hand-dyed wool for the weaving of the patterned cloth. These coverlets are usually dated and inscribed with the name of the weaver and his or her place of residence. The more unusual patterns are considered the most collectible. Prices range considerably. Occasionally, but very rarely so, a coverlet can be picked up for less than $30. A more general starting price is $75, and this can range upward to $150 or more, depending upon where you buy. Coverlets hold particular appeal for those who enjoy extensive research into historical records of coverlet makers and names. Otto Thieme of Madison, Wisconsin, is one such collector. He became a textile researcher-teacher-artist-collector when a girl he was going with during his student days introduced him to textiles through a course she was taking. Today, one of his favorite treasures is a Jacquard coverlet which was bought very inexpensively from an antique dealer and which resulted in five years of detective work. Woven into the coverlet was "John E. Schneider, Hamburg Mo."; this immediately alerted Otto to its rarity, since he knew of only one other weaver from west of the Mississippi. Musty wills, deeds, maps, citizenship papers—Otto studied his way through anything and everything that would provide him with more information about John Schneider. He unearthed twenty extant coverlets and much interesting biographical information, and learned the existence of six other weavers from that part of the country as well.

There are a number of other categories of coverlets, most of them rather rare and oftentimes difficult to identify without some intimate working knowledge of the weaving process. There are the linsey-woolseys, woven with a warp of linen and a weft of homespun wool; there are coverlets woven with the overshot technique that employs a "binder" weft and a pattern weft; there are double-weave coverlets that are very heavy since two separate layers are actually woven at one time; and there are the summer-and-winter coverlets that employ

Homespun coverlet with "American Independence, Declared July 4, 1776, Wove in 1837" woven in each corner. Note the coverlet inside the trundle bed. This coverlet was used by the original owners of Rock Hall, where visitors can see a number of other fine coverlets. This small Nassau County museum serves as a community center for much textile craft activity. On a nice spring morning, you are likely to encounter a group of local women quilting together in the back yard. It is this marriage of past and present which has boosted the vitality of both periods.

yet another weaving technique, though often any reversible coverlet is called by this name.

The Smithsonian Museum of History and Technology in Washington, D.C., has an exhibit that features an early Jacquard loom all set up, as well as many fine coverlets of all types. Many other museums have excellent and interesting collections, and some, such as the Newark Museum in Newark, New Jersey, have issued illustrated publications.

Rugs

Carpets have been esteemed for their beauty and value since the beginning of civilization. It was not until the eighteenth century that anyone would have considered using them on the floor where they would be subject to wear and tear. Instead, rugs were used to give warmth to beds, as tent hangings, or as saddle blankets and bags. Today few homes would be considered furnished without at least one carpet but while the purchase of a rug is an important aspect of home furnishing, in most instances it does not represent a collectible. The three types of carpets which most frequently encompass collecting as well as one-time home furnishings buying are Oriental, North American Indian, and hooked rugs. Antique versions of all three have become harder to obtain and to afford. The increasing importance attached to keeping old skills alive has shown promise of invigorating current production.

ORIENTAL RUGS

Historically, woven carpets of high-quality design and craftsmanship have been traced back as far as the sixth century A.D. A very rare

One of ten Oriental rugs bought at an auction advertised in a German-Jewish newspaper in the early 1940s: The auctions were of possessions that arrived in this country—though their owners did not. Ownership of these rugs represents a special sort of trust.

surviving example is preserved in ice at the Hermitage Museum in Leningrad. According to Preben Liebetrau, author of *Oriental Rugs in Color* (Macmillan, 1963), the existence of this famous rug, known as the Altai carpet, is due to one of those fortuitous accidents of fate: Robbers scavenged a grave for precious metals and stones, leaving the rug behind and along with it an opening which allowed water, which later turned to ice, to seep in.

From these ancient beginnings, carpets have continued to be hand-knotted across a very broad geographic spectrum so that when we speak of an Oriental carpet we encompass the products of the Balkan countries, Turkey, North Africa, the Caucasus, Iran, Afghanistan, India, Turkestan, and China.

It is during the sixteenth century that most of the original master-piece designs which have served as models for subsequent generations of weavers were created. One of the most famous and outstanding of these sixteenth-century masterpieces is the Ardabil carpet in the Victoria and Albert Museum in London.

What about collectibility? Are the more accessible rugs of more recent and future vintage automatically overpriced and not worth collecting, and are all the antiques to be seen only in museums?

The answer to the first question is yes and no. The demand for Oriental carpets, especially since World War II, has been enormous, with production actually lagging behind since potential weavers have been lured to other labor markets. All this has driven the prices of choice rugs up to the point of eliminating the shoestring budget buyer. However, for those willing to pay top prices, there is, as mentioned in the introductory part of this book, the inevitability of death and changing lifestyles to uphold the rotation of ownership. This applies to new as well as old. The antique label on rugs, as on other things, has become increasingly flexible, with any carpet over 50 years old highly valued.

Before you Oriental lovers in the garage-sale price league retreat to looking at the pictures in the mushrooming number of lavishly color-illustrated books on Orientals, take heart. Use those books, buying one or two of the older and less expensive volumes as permanent references, and study the others (which, like the carpets themselves, can be very costly) in the library. Armed with an in-depth understanding of color, design, and workmanship and your own heightened appreciation, you stand a fair chance of making intelligent choices and compromises. Larry Edman, himself a weaver, has been collecting textiles since he was a graduate student not all too long ago. Among his many modestly priced treasures are twenty small Oriental carpets bought at garage sales for $10 to $15 each. While even these low-cost rugs have undoubtedly appreciated in price in the past ten years, this type of collecting imposes none of the decision-making jitters accompanying more lofty investments. A collector like Larry can rely upon his esthetic response since, if he's at all realistic, he knows that a $15 or even a $50 to $100 rug is unlikely to have the value of one selling for hundreds or thousands of dollars.

For absolutely rock-bottom bargain collectors, there are really badly worn rugs with perhaps one good area, like Yvonne Porcella's twenty-five-cent flea market "treasure." Yvonne, who is more of a belt and bag and clothing person (see Chapter 5), does consider anything woven as a possibility for her collection. She feels she would need a rug expert to verify her rug's date and exact origin, though her knowledge of yarns helped her to ascertain that it was genuinely hand-dyed.

What if you don't want to furnish your home with a lot of really distressed and ragged-looking rugs, even if they do contain traces of good design and coloring? My advice is that if you can come close to Yvonne's price, buy it even if there are just a few good inches of weaving. Then cut out that good section—yes, cut it (the Altai carpet is a treasure because it was preserved and in *good* condition), and don't worry about frayed edges. In fact, emphasize the fragmentary appearance with a bit of extra pulling at warp and weft. Then frame your bit of carpet against a white mat, like a Coptic fragment. A collection of such fragments may not be enormously valuable, but it will certainly be handsome and enjoyable.

Since true expertise takes years of study and travel, I strongly urge buyers of choice Orientals to enlist help from those truly in the know. Here are a few general guidelines:

1. Don't try to buy large room-sized rugs on a tiny budget. A small well-designed rug can offer all the visual impact of a large one and while it won't do much in the way of covering your floors, it can make an attractive wall hanging or wall grouping. Once you buy rugs as hangings, you need to be less concerned about strength and durability.

2. Take a cue from the early weavers who used the carpets they wove not only as hangings but as all-purpose pouches. Perhaps a carpet with a few worn spots can be made into a wall pouch or a pillow, with the bad areas turned inward. Many nomadic pouches are still in use though the nomads themselves are finding less need for them and their bags and blankets have become collectibles in and of themselves. (See page 89.)

3. To tell if a rug is hand-knotted or machine-made, try to take hold of a single fiber. If it pulls away easily, it is probably a machine-made product.

4. To get a clear picture of worn or repaired spots, hold the carpet to the light. Also turn the corner inward on a diagonal and tug at it gently. If you hear a crackling sound, you are faced with a rot problem resulting from damp storage.

5. Variations in color are *not* signs of poor craftsmanship but in fact are characteristics of vegetable-dyed fibers. However, many unscrupulous merchants bleach out the colors to fake this look, so

check the back which will show up the harsher, unmasqueraded dyes.

6. Age is very hard to establish. If you buy an expensive rug, try to have a seasoned buyer along.

7. Kilims, or flat-woven rugs, will not have a pile. The weft threads are woven back and forth across the warp threads and where two different colors meet, a slit is formed. These little slits are *not* holes, but characteristic of the technique.

Kashmir or Numdah rugs are not woven at all but felted, a process of pressing moist, unspun fibers together and then decorating the surface with embroidery. Inexpensive contemporary embroidered felt carpets from India have been imported in recent years and with the new interest by contemporary artists in ancient felt- and paper-making processes some of these Numdahs should be more collectible than ever—especially if the collector gives some thought and attention to combining some small rugs with available examples of modern American-made felt forms.

Navajo Rugs

The American Indian has a rich textile heritage: Embroidered and beaded costumes and accessories, patchwork, woven blankets, and rugs. The Navajo rug ranks high as a textile collectible. Its simple and direct design statement and sturdy construction appeal to a wide taste level, and fortunately rug weaving continues to be significantly active today. To be sure, imitations are rampant and the old, aged rugs are harder to obtain and quite expensive. It is the Navajo's traditional desire for anonymity in creative work which has contributed to the rip-offs. Also, since few rug weavers can support themselves with their craft, the incentive to continue the tradition is often weakened by the lure of more profitable industrial jobs. Many young Navajo girls do continue to learn weaving skills, though not always directly from their relatives, since many go to boarding school. Mardel Esping, who teaches in one such school, often takes her students to the rug auctions held by the Crown Point Weaving Association in the heart of New Mexico. She encourages young weavers to sell through the auctions since in this way they will keep 90 percent of the proceeds.

For the collector auctions like this represent an opportunity to purchase quality-controlled Indian rugs in an authentic marketplace. The weavers are themselves present so that it is possible to make personal contacts. Seeing them in their rainbow-colored velvet blouses, full satin skirts, and ancient silver and turquoise brooches affords a textile and jewelry exhibit in itself.

"Don't expect to find the most established weavers at these auctions," Mardel Esping warns. "Those weavers don't have to bring their work to the auctions since they were discovered long ago by the rich and serious collector and their rugs are sold before they even start to weave." The new collector can of course assume that even the master weavers were once undiscovered. The rugs you will find at these auctions, according to Mardel, are good but not museum quality. Each one is labeled with the name and address of the weaver, the fiber content and the type of dye used (Mardel considers the natural-dyed rugs the "sleepers"). The prices are a matter of supply and demand. Mardel has seen them double in the three years since she began her own collection of some twenty rugs.

As with any auction, it is important to arrive well ahead of the scheduled 7 P.M. sale to leave plenty of time for inspection and enjoying the atmosphere. The auctions last from four to six hours, with a rug sold every minute. The sales take place Friday nights at the Crown Point public grade school and you need a car to get there from Albuquerque or Gallup. To write for information see Chapter 8, Organizations.

Each weaver's rug is signed in to be tagged as to type of yarn and dyes used and the weaver's name. All photographs of the Crown Point auctions courtesy of Mardel Esping.

Searching for the "best" rug can involve approximately two hours of concentrated appraisal prior to the auction.

Traditional Two Gray Hills patterns are always popular. A rug is sold approximately every minute for four to six hours.

Rug-hooking is truly a craft of the people—sailors, fishermen, farm women, as well as leisured ladies. Like the patchwork quilt it is notable for its utilization of scraps of fabrics and yarn thrums (the weaver's cutoff yarn ends). The technique itself was probably inspired by the looping evident in ancient weavings.

While the collector of antique hooked rugs usually thinks in terms of examples originating in nineteenth-century America, hooked rugs have been traced back to earliest antiquity—to Denmark, Norway, Ireland, Scotland, and England. These historic evidences are mostly in the form of fragments, interesting studies rather than collectibles.

The nineteenth century marked the real flowering of rug-hooking as a widely practiced functional and self-expressive craft. It took the folk art and crafts movement, though, to elevate the hooked rug to the status of a fine collectible.

Who Collects Hooked Rugs?

The antique hooked rugs have the same naïve charm of many patchwork quilts, and they appeal to the same type of collector. In many instances those who collect quilts will also collect rugs—like Marcia and Ron Spark—though the rug collections tend to be smaller because they are harder to amass. Those who concentrate strictly on the rugs often do intensive research and share their findings by lending their collections, alone or in combination with other people's rugs, to be shown in public places. Others collect as inspiration for creating their own contemporary hooked rugs, which could echo the traditional

The Spark family believes in living with their collectibles and it is the children's room that serves as a rug gallery. The rug with the duck swimming between two flower pots, so reminiscent of a Matisse painting, found its way from New Jersey to Arizona via mail-order buying. Photo Paul Sheldon.

The rug above the toy soldier was made for Art Pugh in Wyoming when he was a small boy. It is dated 1908. The Mary Had A Little Lamb rug is another family favorite and a rarity since people were rarely depicted in old rugs. Photo Paul Sheldon.

motifs or be completely different. A recent issue of the magazine *Spinning Wheel* featured a collector named Maude Zane who took a rug-hooking class in 1956 and has been collecting as well as hooking ever since. She and her husband attend house sales and, living in Pennsylvania as they do, are able to indulge their special liking for Amish and Mennonite rugs. (Maine is another good state for tracking down good and well-priced hooked rugs.) Like many collector-hobbyists, Mrs. Zane has found professional as well as personal satisfaction, since she has become a teacher and demonstrator for the Pennsylvania Farm Museum, Landis Valley, Pennsylvania.

For those who prefer to collect contemporary art, there is much to choose from, for many artists have created fine rug and wall hangings, either all hooked or combining fiber techniques. Designs range from strictly graphic to pictorial.

Following are a few things to remember when buying hooked rugs:

1. Whether you buy from the past or the present, you are likely to run into the more ordinary rugs hooked from commercial patterns. During the mid-nineteenth century, a Maine peddler named Edward Sands Frost cut stencil patterns on metal plates and printed rug designs by the thousands. These patterns were not quite prepackaged with conveniently cut yarns, like today's kits, so you might find some with nice original touches in both design and yarn use.

A *really* choice collectible would be an unworked Frost pattern, and I ran across just one such during the entire course of working on this book.

2. There are three basic types of antique rugs to be found: floral, pictorial, and geometric. The floral type was most popular and common in Victorian times. Some were very elaborate emulations of Aubusson carpets and these, mostly from Canada and New England, are considered most valuable. Of the animal designs, the more unusual creatures are considered most desirable.

3. As with any collectible, dates and names incorporated into the design add to the value, as do indications of any special commemorative purpose.

4. A linen base and very coarse pile can be an indication of age though many current examples are also coarsely piled.

5. Don't expect to find very large rugs. Ovals and half circles used as welcome mats are very common.

6. Study the colors in examples in historic exhibits to absorb their special tones and make comparisons when buying. The earliest rugs were all naturally dyed.

More Household Treasures

While in some parts of the country any fabrics which are not acrylic tend to be considered useless and are priced accordingly (see Chapter 2), in most places the box of goodies for a dollar the lot is likely to be priced by the piece. Good values nevertheless abound for those with a sharp eye and a sense for grouping things with the collector's special sensibility.

HANDKERCHIEFS

Interestingly, that rather humble necessity and long-standing safe gift item, the handkerchief, has enjoyed collectible status for considerable time. Take any commemorative event—political campaign, inauguration, exposition, or fair—and you'll discover a commemorative handkerchief was made in its honor. Popular figures and images seen in books and magazines and on various objects are as likely to appear on a handkerchief. The copperplate prints used to fashion whole-cloth spreads and bed furnishings were also worked into handkerchiefs. In their book, *America's Quilts and Coverlets*, Safford and Bishop picture a privately owned quilt worked around a handkerchief centerpiece entitled "The Death of General Washington." The Henry Ford Museum owns a quilt lined with pieced handkerchiefs of the Declaration of Independence.

The handkerchiefs all by themselves can fetch impressive prices if they are printed with a particularly collectible type of subject. For example, I've seen a "Gone With the Wind" handkerchief priced at

$250. As a general rule, though, you can get together a nice group of unusual and attractive pictorial handkerchiefs for from $2 to $28, depending upon where you buy. Images which were part of magazine illustrations of the 1900s to 1930s period make for a charming specialty. Mary Stinger from Trenton, New Jersey, for example, collects both dolls and textile items so that it was only natural for her to be attracted to handkerchiefs featuring the children drawn by Grace Dayton. Mary bought a couple of handkerchiefs and then researched them, looking for similar illustrations in doll books and old magazines. She found out that Dayton was a well-known New York illustrator of children's books and originator of such paper memorabilia favorites as the Dolly Dingle paper dolls and the even more famous Campbell Soup Kids. These same "Kids" grace the handkerchief Mary lent to me for photography.

Handkerchiefs don't have to have pictorial images to have collecting appeal. In his list of Someday-to-be-Valuables, Otto Thieme (pages 79–80) recommends saving family Communion hankies. Margaret Brown's wedding handkerchief is an important component in a family lace hanging (page 54). Carolanne Rossin of Brooklyn Heights, who runs a shop named Rosycheeks specializing in art deco furnishings, has found that a table of embroidered and lace-edged hankies priced at from 25¢ to a dollar and displayed in old-fashioned glass boxes and cases more than pays for itself. The hankies are "something to buy" even if other items are beyond reach, and bargains when compared to new ones in department stores. As collectibles they can be grouped for

Handkerchief with pictorial image of children from drawings of artist Grace Dayton whose work spanned the period from 1909 to 1936. From the collection of Mary E. Stinger.

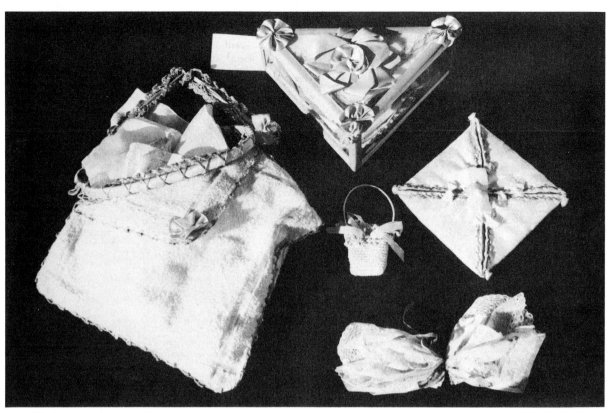

Dainty hankies, attractively displayed in old-fashioned glass and fabric cases more than earn their keep in an antique establishment. This grouping was photographed at Rosycheeks, New York.

greater interest and value: hankies with initials to match the collector's name; colored hankies, specific types of floral embroidery motifs, etc. With some recent newspaper fashion writers headlining stories like "A Comeback for Lacy Hankies" (*The New York Times*), Rosycheeks and other shops are sure to keep those hankie tables well stocked.

If you'd like to display your collection in one of those old glass hankie boxes, they're likely to cost a good bit more than their contents. However, since the originals were usually homemade, you can follow in this tradition, taking some shortcuts such as the use of ribbons with a stick-on side.

The supplies needed are ordinary windowpane glass, a small glass cutter, cardboard, the edging ribbon or tape, plus decorative bows or trimmings.

Here are the step-by-step procedures adapted from a woman's magazine of years ago:

1. Make a model by cutting out cardboard pieces. The box seen in the picture of the hankie table requires two triangles and three rectangular pieces for the sides.
2. Place the glass to be cut on top of a flat, padded surface; the cardboard pattern on top of the glass. Glass cutters usually include

instructions for use. The whole trick is to hold the wheel firmly against the edge of the cardboard pattern, which acts as a ruler. Roll the wheel over the glass surface so that it is scored rather than cut, enabling you to break off the unwanted portion of glass.

3. When all the pieces for the box have been cut, lay those to be joined in position and cut the stick-on ribbon so that half covers the edge of each piece, forming a hinge. When all the inside hinges have been attached, repeat for the outside. The lift-up sides of the box top will have the ribbon running from the top edge and down around the bottom. Use extra glass and ribbon to try out rectangular, square, or even hexagonal shapes.

PILLOWCASES AND TABLE COVERS

Some household linens you inherit are valuable primarily for their personal sentiment. Today's servantless homes mandate usage for only the most special occasions, or not at all. Thus those who own these old things and treasure them, find new and less-demanding display uses or get rid of them, making them available to those who are not put off by the care involved or who are inspired to create a practical new form of display.

Larry Edman's taste encompasses a wide range of textiles and like a true collector he gathers together enough examples in each area of interest to make for an interesting representation. In addition to his already described Oriental carpets, he has some thirty pieces each of Peruvian and ikat weavings, and some thirty-five embroidered pillow covers and table runners. The latter are all in the same basic style of silk or cotton floss on linen, from the 1800s to about 1920. Many of the pillowcases were sold as do-it-yourself embroidery kits, and some are only partially worked, showing the painted or stenciled designs. One has particular personal significance since it is embroidered with the name of his home state, Kansas. The cost of the pillow collection ranges from 50¢ to $10 apiece.

My own collection of household embroideries is a bequest from a talented and prolific grandmother. I agree with Bucky King that a beautifully made piece of work in good condition should not be cut up. If you can't find a way to mount it or use it, or don't want to store it, give it to a university or museum textile collection, but don't destroy it. However, on occasion I feel an alteration which does not involve cutting but which gives a new image is worthwhile. My Richelieu lace panel could have been mounted against black cloth, but since I have white cornices overlapping the windows of my dining room and knew the material was of sturdy fabrication, I decided to dye the panel in black liquid Rit dye. The effect is a striking silhouette hanging, which has lost its tablecloth look, but none of its basic beauty. I would not recommend this dye treatment for fragile textiles!

Richelieu lace table runner made by the author's grandmother, circa 1928. The lace was recently dipped, into black dye to create a silhouette hanging.

Antimacassars, Doilies, and Other Lacelike Treasures

Not long ago *The New York Times* published a photograph showing one of its columnists, William Safire, interviewing members of the Standing Committee of the National People's Congress in China. Interviewer and interviewees were seated in armchairs draped both across the back and arms with filet crochet antimacassars and doilies. China may be one of the remaining strongholds where these crochet items are being used as originally intended. Far more frequently these reminders of needlewomen's patience and dexterity are being hauled out of storage and proudly displayed under glass, incorporated into contemporary clothing and even copied by the ever-swelling throngs of do-it-yourself fiber enthusiasts. In 1976 the Center for the History of American Needlework mounted an exhibit entitled "The Art of the Doily," at the Port Authority Bus Terminal in New York City, in honor of International Women's Year, and this was so well received that it has been traveling around the country on loan ever since. (See Chapter 8, Organizations.)

The adaptability and availability of old crocheted and knitted pieces at prices which are still very affordable makes them one of the fastest-growing areas of collectibles. Other types of lacework can still be had cheaply too, mainly because most antique store owners can't tell one type of lace from another. When I asked John Block of Sotheby Parke Bernet's PB Eighty-Four auction gallery what types of textiles they did not do much with now but expected to be more interested in sooner or later, the answer was "lace." And so, lace lovers, *now* is the time to pick up what you can!

What to Do with What You've Got

In spite of the renewed appreciation of fine workmanship, people continue to ponder the question of what to do with what they've got. Not every doily or tablecloth is worth displaying as wall art. What's more, today's high-cost living spaces severely restrict display areas. For many this very problem has opened the door to a whole new kind of collecting: collecting to recycle. This gives a whole new life to what was formerly dead storage. Recycling has attracted the attention of some enormously talented fabric artists but it is also possible to effect major visual and functional transformations with minimal skills. The dyeing of my grandmother's lace (along with a handkerchief case now used as an evening bag) can be equated to a bit of sanding to resuscitate a piece of old furniture. All my changes have been effected with basic sewing, knotless netting (a fancy name for the buttonhole stitch), crochet, or knitting.

A Boxful of "Oddments" and How They Were Used and Reused

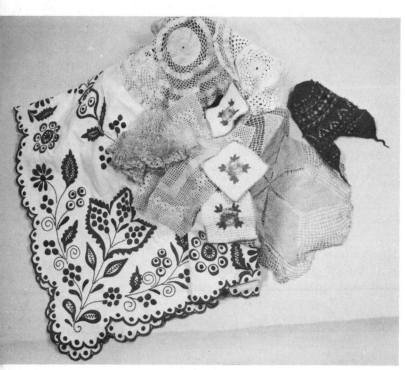

Pictured here are the contents of a box of partially inherited and partially flea market-acquired pieces. The embroidered tablecloth was made in the 1920s and is in perfect condition except for some stains which I decided to regard as part of the antique patina, as per my conservator friend Michael Bogle's advice about removal versus nonremoval of spots. Some of the doilies are a rectangular filet pattern popular during the 1930s and often available in matching sets, which makes them very adaptable for clothing construction. The potholders are probably no older than the 1940s but at 20¢ each they were worth buying just to use for their rose centers or to build a fun collection of kitchen textiles. The South American knitted hat was bought at a street fair for a dollar, mainly for its intricate knit designs and French knot embroidery.

Here are some of the doilies from the box of oddments made into a blouse, a matching clutch bag, and a pendant necklace. The blouse is constructed from four rectangular doilies with crochet used to join and edge, the number of rows depending upon the size of the wearer. The bag is lined with a piece salvaged from a log cabin "cutter" quilt; it is made from a single doily folded into an envelope with a crocheted loop and crochet-covered button. Two other blocks from the old quilt were sewn into a pillow, and appliquéd with a pair of rag dolls found at a flea market for a dollar. The necklace was made from a torn doily. Single crochet stitches turned a narrow strip of the doily into a neckband, and are worked around the pendant and onto its surface to encase a small handdrawn pebble. The plant hanger? That's the South American hat, minus ear flaps, lined with a plastic grocery container, and hung by long crochet chains.

What better way to frame an old family picture than with a piece of old lace? If you're going to follow my procedures on this, don't use any valuable lace. Here's how the frame was made: The photograph, a silver anniversary photo of my great-grandmother and family, was carefully mounted onto a piece of half-inch-thick styrofoam, leaving a mat-sized border all around. An old thin lace placemat was placed on waxed paper, and brushed on both sides with a mixture of half white glue and water. The picture was placed face up in the center and the sides folded around. A coating of glue and water mixture over the photo provides a clear protective finish, making glass unnecessary. When the glue-water mixture dries, the lace will be quite firm. The roses in each corner are the centers from the potholders in the box of oddments. The styrofoam base enabled me to pin rather than sew them in place with clear colored pins. The old shade-pull hanger is stitched in place with a French knot.

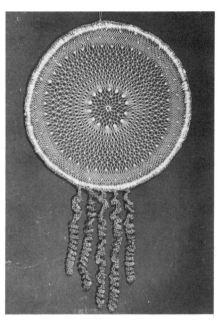

This beautiful doily is enjoying a new life as a window hanging. The hoop and shiny copper cord used to recycle it are the result of auxiliary buying trips to flea markets, where the hoops were being sold at five cents apiece and the cord sold on 50¢ spools by someone who had bought out odd lots from a cordage store. The doily was pinned around the hoop, then secured with blanket stitches. The dangling additions are optional, made with an easy adaptation of the basic single crochet stitch: Make a long chain and crochet back along it by making three stitches, instead of the usual one, into every chain.

Sally Kinsey illustrates that the doily antimacassar school of fashion can have the classic simplicity suitable for any age or taste. Her doily panel is built out with cotton slub string worked in quick double crochet stitches, with single crochets for the edges.

The rear view reveals an antimacassar shawl collar trimmed with Victorian beads and buttons. The entire tunic cost $5.

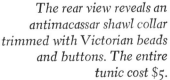

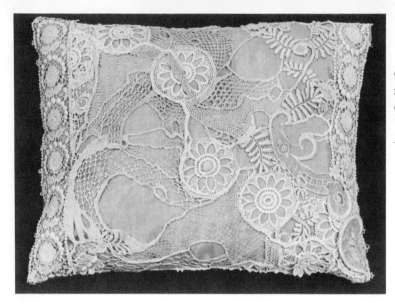

Old lace and new lace are combined into a functional collage which owner-designer Otto Thieme calls "Memories of a Grandmother's Youth." Photograph, John Barsness.

More Mounting Ideas

As already mentioned earlier, linens and laces can be framed like any picture, simply mounted on contrasting fabric-covered boards, or tacked directly to an appropriate backing, such as a window cornice. Some things, especially lace, deserve to be seen from both sides and there are several solutions to this. Stretching the form inside a supporting frame like the previously illustrated hoop is one way. Attaching the lace to the front of a frame and backing it with a reflecting mirror is another. Another method is to sandwich the lace between two sheets of plexiglass, drill holes through the corners, and suspend from the ceiling. I also frame batiks this way.

Yet another way of mounting lace is to stitch it, collage fashion, into a pillowcase, backing it with a contrasting liner.

The Best of Both Worlds: The New/Antique Hanging

Suppose you are not even minimally handy with needle and hook, or the idea of making something new out of something old simply does not appeal to you? And suppose that while you love old things you do also like the idea of collecting from living artists?

There *is* a way to have your cake, or should I say old fabric. A lot of fabric and fiber artists also like old things and incorporate them into their work. Some will do commissions which will utilize your own accumulations or theirs. I've already touched upon this in talking about bicentennial quilts made with old fabrics. The following illustrations of the work of three artists working in this new-old genre will give the reader an idea of the wide range of effects possible.

The habit of collecting textiles was passed on to Susanna Lewis by a grandmother who all her life cut and snipped bits and pieces of whatever she liked from the personal and household goods other members of the family were about to throw out. Sometimes she'd cut an especially nice collar off a dress, other times a pocket, or that portion which contained a date or name or other identifying mark. She also saved baby hats, hankies, pieces of yardage, and hand- and machine-made flowers. As in many families, the saving habit often skips a generation, which accounts for much of the stuff in thrift-shop bins. That's how Susanna came to rescue her grandmother's gatherings from her mother's trash heap. As she puts it, "I felt an obligation to my two daughters to *do* something with all that family history." And so she appliquéd a five-generation-spanning collection into a 42-inch-by-11-foot hanging. Her mother, delighted to have what was formerly just a lot of seemingly useless stuff so beautifully assembled, now proudly displays this single piece of "fuss and sentiment" in an otherwise starkly modern house.

Five generations of doilies, collars, and baby caps on handspun linen towels. Note the daguerreotype at the lower left-hand corner. Assembled by Susanna E. Lewis; owned by June and Stanford Erickson.

Margaret and Bradley Brown's collected laces are assembled into an appliquéd and quilted hanging by Susanna Lewis. The handkerchief in the upper left-hand corner was crocheted by Mrs. Brown's grandmother, given to her as a high school graduation gift (1956) to be used on her wedding day, which took place ten years later. The second collar from the top was worn by Mrs. Brown's grandmother as a child. The edgings and other items were collected by an aunt from Bradley Brown's side of the family.

Susanna Lewis collects laces to study and to use. These examples of mid-nineteenth century bobbin lace, copies of seventeenth-century netting, are handsome enough to mount and frame as is.

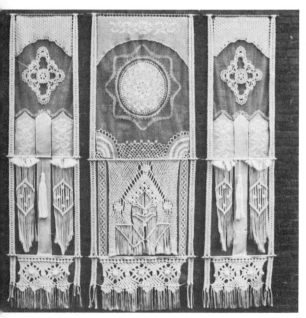

Easy care new-old lace curtains designed for three windows in a Victorian brownstone. Susanna employed knitting, crochet, macrame, and bobbin lace techniques in nylon yarn on nylon net. Collection of Amy Solomon.

They are even more effective as part of a "Tree of Life" hanging which includes quilting, appliqué, crochet, and lace knitting. From the collection of Eleanor and John Dimoff.

Not every family is fortunate enough to claim a member with Susanna Lewis' vision and ability, so it's lucky that she uses her talents professionally as well as privately. She has assembled a lace collection from both sides of Margaret and Bradley Brown's family into an appliquéd and quilted hanging, and translated a "Tree of Life" Currier and Ives print owned by Eleanor and John Dimoff into a hanging to which she added some of her own antique bobbin-lace doilies. Susanna has also executed commissions for window panels in traditional bobbin lace, macramé, knitting, and crochet techniques, made with easy-care nylon.

Windowscapes by Judy Dodds

Judy Dodds has had a varied career. After a stint as a museum curator she designed and sold patchwork kits for children and this in turn led her to experiment with designs for wall hangings reflecting the scenes seen inside and outside the windows of her Vermont surroundings. The hangings are a perfect outlet for Judy's lifelong passion for old crocheted items, quilts, towels, and fabrics. Unlike the serious quilt collector she looks for the "cutter" variety, and one of her all-time fortuitous buys was a rummage-sale crazy quilt signed and dated "E. H. Marble–1899." The hanging into which this was stitched is now owned by the Vermont Marble Company of Proctor, Vermont.

"Tea Tray," measuring 32" × 48", contains a real crochet tea cosy, circa 1900, a tea napkin, circa 1930 and a 1920s' print fabric for the background—all squirreled away among Judy Dodds' family belongings.

Diana Willner is an avid collector of old laces and fabrics and also not very old or valuable fabric items which in her talented hands take on a much more collectible character. She uses some of the doilies, tablecloths, and lace trims crocheted by her mother during World War II while her father was in the army, but is saving some specifically for a family collage.

Diana Willner's new-old antique hangings tend toward the three-dimensional, like this piece combining old printed fabrics, a curtain pull, bits of lace, antique molding, and some of Diana's own very imaginative crochet additions.

Here is an assortment of bits and pieces from different periods, to be used eventually for a Willner collage. The printed fabric is from a Japanese bathrobe of recent vintage, the black lace comes from a dress once worn by Diana's great-grandmother, the patchwork is from an unfinished friendship quilt, the ribbons are antique, and the dark printed pieces at the front are the remainders of an authentic paisley shawl. (See page 14 for a choice condition paisley.)

Though even the everyday sort of needlework, like the household doily, has today become interesting enough to display, most needlework throughout history has been basically utilitarian, no matter how decorative its execution. There have been some exceptions to this, notably pictorial embroideries and samplers, most made by young schoolgirls for whom the mastery of needlework was a prerequisite for being well-educated.

It was during the seventeenth century in England that embroidery as a decorative rather than a functional art came to full fruition, and it is the work of this period that has long been the stuff of fine collections, with auction prices recorded as ranging from several hundred to thousands of dollars. Stumpwork, a type of padded, three-dimensional embroidery used for boxes as well as pictures (including coffins!) was a particular specialty and whenever an example becomes available through an estate sale, it is invariably featured as an important attraction in the sale announcements.

The sampler made by very young girls, first as a record of stitches to be used in their adult roles as housewives responsible for marking and identifying household belongings, and later simply as a record of their achievements, is probably the best-known type of nonutilitarian stitchery. Collecting affords enormous variety. There are samplers from a broad geographic and historical spectrum, with many interestingly differentiated themes and styles. Like so much that is today recognized as folk art, the sampler was long in the category of "curiosity," not to be taken too seriously since it was after all "just the work of youngsters." Those old enough and smart enough to appreciate the sampler's charm and worth way back then were able to build interesting and diversified collections for very little money. In an article written for *Antiques* in June 1923, for example, Mrs. Harold E. Gillingham described some of her adventures as a sampler collector. She recalled with particular pride a purchase of one dated 1810 for the princely sum of six shillings! Today's sampler enthusiast will have to search very hard to find much of anything dated late eighteenth or early nineteenth century, and prices, while not sky-high as valuable collectibles go, are certainly a far cry from six shillings. As with everything considered so far, the opportunities for pleasurable and rewarding collecting even within the tightest budgets still exist. The trick once again is to take an open-minded approach to what is worthwhile in terms of provenance and condition. If a sampler is frayed and unframed but of interesting design and authentic antiquity, why not treat it as a fragment, as already suggested for low-budget Oriental rug lovers? The fact that it is not framed may actually be an advantage, for old framed samplers invariably present conservation problems since the acids from a frame's wooden backboard may cause the cloth to rot. More than likely, an unframed sampler in poor condition has already been removed from its frame to prevent further damage.

Eighteenth-century samplers, dated and signed and in prime condition, are most likely to be found in museum collections—like this one, dated 1780 and signed CWB. It hangs in one of the bedrooms of historic Rock Hall, Lawrence, New York.

Another sampler photographed at Rock Hall. This one is particularly rare. It contains the Ten Commandments embroidered in French by a twelve-year-old girl and is dated 1726. Foreign-language samplers made in America are considered by most to be authentic only if the provenance is firmly established—as is the case here, since Rock Hall has been occupied by only two owners, the Martins and the Hewletts, before passing into county ownership.

If you are collecting less valuable samplers from more recent years, you can make your collection special and more valuable by searching out variations of the commonplace—names and dates which relate to you personally or to other objects in your possession. You can gather together a special grouping of alphabet samplers, scattered motif samplers, house samplers, or one of each. This enables you to mix bargains with an occasional "splurge" item which will invest the entire group with a special touch. Many sampler designs were taken from published patterns, so if you can find some of these and collect them as a unit with actual samplers, you are creating still another kind of distinctive unit.

WHO COLLECTS SAMPLERS?

Most sampler collectors are also students of historic needlework. Many museums and historical societies have fine sampler collections for perusal. There are also many handsomely illustrated and scholarly books available and a number of these, sad for the authors but luckily for the collectors, are available at greatly reduced or remaindered prices, which makes the books alone worth collecting. While samplers, especially American-made ones, have had their followers for many years, there are many collectors who have joined the ranks fairly recently. Norma Papish of Bethesda, Maryland, acquired her first sampler after becoming a docent at the Smithsonian Institution's Museum of History and Technology just six years ago. This volunteer position expanded her interest in needlework to the point that she developed a special tour which has become one of the best *free* mini-tours in the country. Every Tuesday morning at 10:15, from November to April, Norma or another Smithsonian docent will take anyone who meets her beneath the big American flag on a guided tour of some of the needlework highlights of the museum. Some truly outstanding samplers and needlework pictures (also done by young girls) are included.

Norma Papish's first sampler was old, dated, and in very poor condition, but then it only cost $10. For her second sampler purchase, again an old one but in better condition, Norma splurged to the tune of $30. Both purchases were made in local antique shops.

Susanna Lewis, whose beautiful lace assemblages and hangings were shown in the previous section, also finds time in her busy schedule as an artist to do museum volunteer work at the Brooklyn Museum, which boasts a fine costume, fabric, and lace collection. Her museum connection has brought many satisfactions, including a tip about the availability of some old and rare knitting samplers in a Manhattan gallery. These samplers are long, bandage-like affairs containing a different pattern every couple of inches, sometimes as many as a hundred or more per roll. Susanna treasures her own sampler and is also translating the one acquired by the museum into a graphed instruction

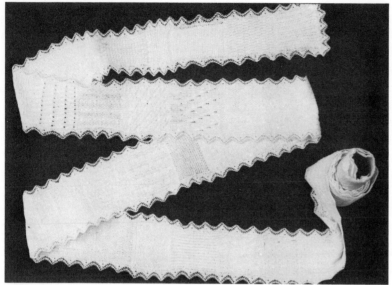

Knitting samplers, unlike the embroidered variety, were not made for framing, but were instead worked in long, narrow rolls, with a different pattern every few inches. This sampler is from the collection of Susanna E. Lewis.

booklet which will be available for purchase to anyone interested in learning to do fancy knitting.

The Berlin patterns which began to be published in profusion in the mid-nineteenth century were the forerunners of our present-day needlepoint kits. They turned the schoolgirl sampler into primarily adult busywork. There has been considerable effort to revive creative sampler-making, but the best examples of these are made by people for their own families and are not usually available—at least not yet. At any rate, the true derivatives of the more inventive and original samplers of the past are found in the creative stitchery which has gone beyond the limits of patterns and has resulted in a whole new art

The true derivative of the very best kind of sampler is the contemporary free-form stitchery. Here is a piece by B. J. Adams, one of the Washington area artists Norma Papish collects along with antique samplers. Photograph taken at the Torpedo Factory, Alexandria, Virginia.

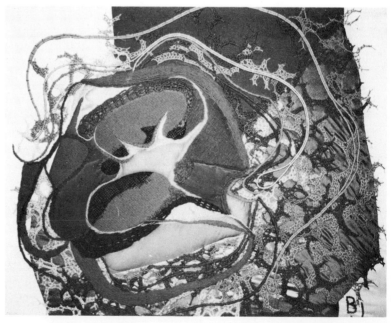

form. The woman most often mentioned as being responsible for setting the hobbyist free from patterns and rigidity is the late Mariska Karasz. It is thus not random eclecticism when Norma Papish collects not only old samplers but the stitcheries of the many fine artists working in the greater Washington, D.C. area. This geographic limitation keeps her collection within financially manageable bounds as well as making it particularly meaningful. She owns a piece by B. J. Adams (page 60) as well as one by Karasz, whose pieces have skyrocketed in price since her death in 1963, something typical of most collecting. Bucky King tells of a lady who bought something from her and who regularly calls to inquire after her health; and as Bucky speculates with amusement, "probably to check on her investment."

Clothing

When John F. Kennedy was inaugurated as President of the United States, his mother, who could certainly afford a new dress, chose an evening gown she had worn forty years earlier. It is the enduring chic of fine clothes which has always been cited as a defense for their high prices. While the original impulse for buying used clothes usually stems from a desire to save rather than to spend, it is the uniqueness and quality which truly account for the boom in their sale. "Antique" in this field has moved closer and closer to the present, with vintage World War II clothing already making room for the hand-embellished denim clothes and T-shirts of the sixties and onward.

Is Clothing a Valid Collectible?

Not only is the public eagerly buying the clothing offered in more and more antique and thrift shops, but it is responding with enthusiastic appreciation to museum and gallery exhibits of apparel from every period and influence—from Parisian designers, to unknown folk artists, to contemporary signed and handmade things. Whatever era or type of design appeals to you, clothing is indeed a valid collectible, with you the collector serving as a movable display armature.

If you have a bent for recycling, the old clothes need not even be in good condition or of a design that was ever considered especially great. We've already seen some recycling done by using clothing items to make wall hangings and to make nonclothing items into wearables. One can of course improve upon the old without ever changing the basic function, as we shall see a bit further on.

Where to Find Old Clothing

The place to start, as with all functional textiles, is in your own and your friends' and relatives' closets—the ones where things "too good to throw out" are stored. Spread the word that you are interested in collecting clothes and will give them the care, attention, and display they deserve. This is likely to bring you some donations, for as Sally Kinsey, who collects for the costume collection of Syracuse University, puts it, "most elderly folks when faced with mortality want objects they have saved to have a secure home."

Flea markets, thrift shops, house sales, and antique shops are all good sources. The shop especially geared to antique clothing is likely to be most expensive, but also stocked with the widest assortment and anything in need of repairs is likely to have been taken care of already. The further you are willing to go to scout for good buys—out-of-the-way country shops and tag sales, and even foreign countries—the closer you will be to the sources used by professional dealers. Many dealers do in fact start out as collectors themselves and go into business to dispose of their collecting excesses. This can be done in the form of a shop or once-in-a-while selling at flea markets.

Clothing can also be bought through the mail, via small ads in antique magazines or small-town weeklies, pretty much the same procedure used by Marcia and Ron Spark in their quilt search. The fact that a number of clothing specialists regularly have ads in the classified sections should be sufficient evidence that they bring results.

There are as many kinds of garments to collect as there are places to find them. Following are some of my favorites among the many wonderful fashions seen in private and public collections. Still more can be seen in Chapter 5.

Very beautiful and well-preserved dresses of this century are often found in shops featuring miscellaneous antiques along with old clothes. Pot Pourri on Atlantic Avenue in Brooklyn opened in 1976 with mostly furniture, but has been devoting most of its window and floor space to clothing.

Pot Pourri's owner, Lynne Parker, like many dealers, is her own best customer. The shop is a perfect way to collect without going broke. For the collector looking for a specialty, kimonos offer great variety as to origin, designs, and prices (see Bucky King's nineteenth-century mandarin coat in Chapter 3). Japanese kimonos are greatly valued and a recent loan exhibition from that country to the National Gallery in Washington caused a considerable stir.

Syracuse University owns a virtual treasure trove of mid-nineteenth century through 1930s costumes, mostly donated by local people, but until Sally Kinsey interested herself in the collection, much of it was uncatalogued and uncared for. Today, it is once again actively exhibited and used by textile students and teachers. The exhibitions in turn have brought new donations.

This black velvet costume, accessorized with ecru lace and a beaded evening purse, was made at a Syracuse couture shop circa 1900 and donated by the W. R. Salisbury family. Courtesy Syracuse University photo service; student model, "Lee."

Men's clothing tends to be less expensive than women's and good buys can be found, especially in things primarily costume. The man behind the camera for most of the pictures in this book, for example, owns a very impressive admiral's jacket bought at a roadside flea market for 50¢ (the buttons alone are worth more!). Here, Bruce Havens, administrator of the Syracuse costume collection, poses in a fully accessorized gentleman's ensemble. Photo, courtesy Syracuse University's Photo Service.

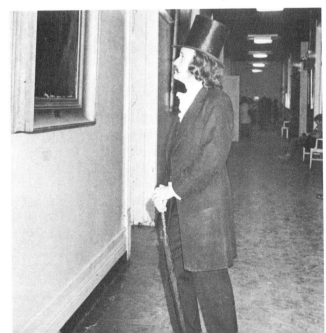

Nancy Lipe marches to a different drummer. She loves the dark, lush, sometimes eery finery of the Victorian era. She's also fortunate in having a mother who is an inveterate house-sale shopper where she bought this black silk mourning bodice which Nancy wears over leotards for very special occasions, but displays most of the time draped over a crochet-covered mannequin.

Nancy Lipe's recycling skills take a decided practical turn when she uses her crochet hook to create variously sized circles to appliqué to a thrift-shop bathrobe. The three-quarter sleeves were extended by adding crochet cuffs. (See Chapter 7 for recycling techniques.)

In Queen Victoria's day no woman was considered properly ready for marriage unless she was "kirked" in a paisley shawl. The embroidered silk and fringed variety was actually made as a piano drape. If you're fortunate enough to own one of these and want to convert it into an elegant tunic as Dee Weber did, fold the square so that the points fall at the front and back of the body. Cut a slit for the neck opening and hem. About 24 inches up from each side of the points, sew the front and back together for about 10 inches or until you get to the base of the armhole. Voilà! Of course, you can just fold the shawl in half and drape it "as is."

Costume and Boudoir Accessories

One of the realities of antique clothing is perhaps best summed up in Bucky King's explanation of why she never makes her recycled garments in anything larger than a size 14: "Regretfully, queen-sized people are not suited to elaborate fabric decoration. The size of their bodies dictates plain fabrics, simple lines, simple everything."

Many collectors actually prefer concentrating on the myriad costume and boudoir accessories available from the past as well as the present. I've already talked about handkerchiefs. Let us also consider bags, gloves, fans, pincushions, and hats and ties, which are readily available for very modest outlays of cash and very considerable pleasures. They make attractive displays, even in small apartments. Their easy portability adds to their appeal for those often on the move.

In terms of usability as well as collectibility, bags probably top the list and readers will be interested to know that men carried small, tape-closed bags, many of bargello needlepoint, as early as the eighteenth century. These, while not as easily obtainable as beaded bags, are around. I was recently shown a boxful of over twenty variously worked fabric bags, including several eighteenth-century bargello types —with a tag of $400 attached to the lot. Also, contemporary artists are creating many fantastic bags which are well worth considering as part of a collection.

Pincushions are still an important accessory for any needlewoman, though no longer as vital to everyday life as they once were. During the fifteenth century pins were such a precious commodity that they were carefully kept in silver boxes, and it was only to have some easily accessible on one's dressing table that the cushion evolved as a holder. By the time Queen Elizabeth reigned, elaborate pincushions were considered highly prized possessions and acceptable gifts for almost any occasion. The Victorian era brought the pincushion to its apex in terms of sheer volume of production and elaborateness of design. Until the recent reevaluation of Victoriana, pincushions were considered by many to typify the worst excesses of that period. Today collectors treasure them for their charm and many people who bought them as interesting curiosities for a dollar or two now find themselves with a collection of miniature soft sculptures. Prices are still reasonable enough to add to or begin one's acquisitions.

Fans, though less utilitarian than the pincushion for present-day lifestyles, have been established collectibles for a long time. Since the fabrics tend to deteriorate, they are often collected for their handles. To the serious collector those of greatest interest were produced between 1860 and 1910 by the Edmond Soper Hunt and Allen Fan companies. If you're lucky enough to own some old fabric fans, treat them gently by avoiding unnecessary opening and closing. In the same category with fans, we have parasols. These have made a functional and fashionable comeback as a result of publicity about the harmful effects of the sun. Rich and fashionable women as well as teenagers collect and use parasols in all colors. Travelers like to bring back samples from different parts of the world.

Accessories photographed in an eighteenth-century bedroom at Rock Hall, Lawrence, New York: A bargello canvas bag with tape closing, probably used by a man as a wallet; a painted canvas hankie case; hankie and old books. Yarn winders, as well as spinning wheels and looms, were likely to be found in several rooms of the house.

More accessories displayed in various bedrooms at Rock Hall: Lace evening mittens and fan, lace handkerchief, an embroidered, a needlepointed, and a beaded pincushion. Victorian beaded pincushions often contain dates and/or names of places.

Beaded pincushions and bags are probably easier to find than an all-beaded hat, like this circa 1930 beauty owned and modeled by Nancy Lipe. Nancy always manages to add some just right personal touch to her favorite things; in this case three fabric roses made from antique velvet and silk. These roses were a popular do-it-yourself accessory in the 1930s. To make one: Fold a strip of fabric 5 inches long and one inch wide in half, coil into a petal and gather the ends together with a tacking stitch.

Here we see an early example of "throw-away chic," a velvet-covered, silk-trimmed cardboard powder box used around 1910 as a dance compact. If you find any of these, they're not likely to be expensive and would make a nice oddity within a bag or box collection. Photo, K. Benzel, Syracuse University Costume Collection.

Meet a Bag Collector

Marilyn Green supports herself as a research librarian, sustains her creative spirit with stitchery necklaces, and indulges her romantic nature by collecting bags, mostly very small ones. She loves wondering where the lovely old beaded purses have been. "I see them twirling from ladies' arms at fancy-dress balls, like Vivien Leigh dancing with Clark Gable in *Gone With The Wind*," Marilyn confides. She collects mostly beaded Victorian bags, tracing her love of beads back to her Michigan childhood when she spent summers bent over the shores of Lake Michigan with a strainer looking for Indian beads, some of which she still has. Marilyn finds bags made with steel and tiny glass beads most available, with charming pictorial and geometric designs, at prices ranging from $8 to $35. "They *can* still be found in excellent condition, like my own favorite find—a red geometric patterned bag, a steal at $10." This, incidentally, is her top price. Besides the bag itself and its inherent romantic mystery, what Marilyn likes best is its clasp. "Almost none are duplicates. You can't imagine the number of variations!"

Being a researcher, she has investigated her subject thoroughly. She can tell you that the Victorian reticules were sometimes called *ridicules*; that when people carried little money purses called miser's purses looped over their belts thieves were said to have carried scissors to clip off the ends; and when making beaded clutch purses was in vogue, ladies used to send their finished beadwork off to Tiffany's in New York to be mounted on cast gold and silver frames.

Most collectors have at least one inherited item to start them off. This Victorian beaded bag, lined in satin with fabric rosebuds around the rim and a silver frame was given to Marilyn Green by her grandmother.

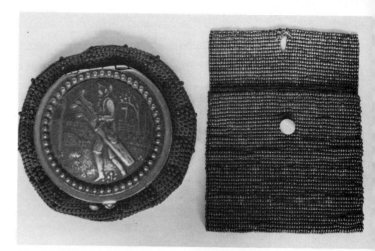

Two prize purchases: At left is an English bag to hold a golf ball. It has a crocheted bottom, steel beadwork, a metal lid with caddie design, and was bought at a flea market for a dollar. At right is the kid-lined clutch bag bought through an ad in Hobbies. Marilyn says it feels the best to hold of all her bags.

Marilyn rotates the bags she collects along with the bags and soft jewelry she makes on a white wall—near a window but NOT in direct sunlight. The influence of one activity upon the other makes it hard to tell which is which. This photo and all others of Marilyn Green's bags by John K. Stimpson.

Where does a collector like Marilyn with a $10 top limit buy most of her bags? She finds thrift shops her best source, though she considers that one of the best things she ever did was to place an ad in the magazine *Hobbies*. This netted her some true gems: two never-used purses; one a circa 1900 child's purse made in Czechoslovakia, and a small steel-beaded envelope purse lined in pure kid, both for $6. Another treasure was a collection of beads used to make purses, with the beads on their original threads with price tags attached (5¢). Marilyn finds the beads wonderful little works of art in themselves and hopes one day to weave them into some sort of contemporary nostalgia bag.

For the beginning collector, Marilyn offers the following tips and precautions:

1. Watch out for rust in the steel purses; also, torn threads on glass beads.
2. Expect silk linings to be disintegrated, like the silk in crazy quilts. If the beads are good, it's easy to put in a new lining.
3. If you're handy, consider handles without bags, and add your own fabric and fiber additions.
4. Bright light can disintegrate delicate beads. A bag collection looks lovely hung inside a window, but its life is approximately two years. (Author's Note: If you'd like to start your own collection with a handmade Victorian-style purse, see the section in Chapter 7, Recycling and Reproduction Skills.)

And Don't Forget About Men's Neckties

Ties have much of the impact and appeal of quilts. They were frequently the one touch of color and personal self-expression in otherwise drab attire, as quilts represented brightness in often austere lives. There has been some interest among recyclers in using ties to make skirts, handbags, and quilts, but for the most part, people tend to erupt in gales of merriment at the idea of saving ties, much less buying old ones. This attitude places them among the best truly cheap fabric collectibles around.

Tie collecting lends itself to many subspecialties. Ron Spark concentrates upon ties of the 1944 to 1951 period. He relates very intimately to these since they represented for him a small measure of self-expression at a time of his life when he was more or less in uniform as an intern. Those bright ties buoyed his spirit as they had been intended to buoy the spirits of people living in that period. "Those ties are sort of dream things," Ron reflects. "For me they were a chance to collect those dreams even on an intern's severely restricted budget. For a couple of dollars spent in a thrift shop I was able to have all the excitement and pleasure experienced later as a quilt collector."

The tie collection does in fact coordinate very well with the larger

Ties can be pieced as seen in this bedspread in the Spark home. Dr. Ron Spark began collecting 1944–1951 vintage ties when in the "uniform" of an intern. Photo Paul Sheldon.

and more impressive quilt collection he and his wife Marcia have amassed. At a recent charity ball quilt show, the Sparks also hung some ties like banners around a rotunda. Unlike quilts which have escalated in price since Ron first started buying them, the ties continue to be available at thrift-shop rates with a recent acquisition of fifteen beautiful new additions totaling $3. In addition to the ties, Ron also owns a tie bedcover and a tie-patched smoking jacket bought for $6 in an antique shop, where it seemed to be waiting for its rightful owner (see page 34).

Baskets

The main news about basket collecting is the fever-pitch intensity amid the swelling ranks. There is an enormously expanded awareness of the diverse origins of baskets (to many, basket collecting once meant North American Indian baskets only), and the development of a whole new category, the contemporary art basket. This last is the university- and workshop-trained artist's reinterpretation of the spontaneously invented, serviceable containers made by primitive people since time immemorial.

For the dedicated folk art collector nothing but an authentic basket from an Indian or equivalent culture will do. For the modernist, the explosion in the craft by newly oriented basketmakers offers a fresh chance to collect objects which provide a meaningful link between the past, present, and future.

GETTING STARTED

One would be hard pressed to find a home, no matter how modest, which does not contain at least several baskets of one kind or another, from plastic, mass-produced laundry baskets to decorative containers bought to hold magazines, dried flowers, yarns, or to lug home a variety of goodies picked up during a holiday. The transition from accumulator of functional containers to collector is usually marked by a mounting curiosity about the baskets' intrinsic form, color, and pattern. The collector knows if a basket is coiled, twined, or woven and is attuned to its mystical role in ceremonial rites and customs. Collecting know-how also brings an expanded view of function, a view that accepts a basket's usefulness whether it's just deep enough to accommodate the tip of a finger or large enough to hold goods to bring to and from a marketplace. The recognition of the relationship to hat forms, masks, and ceremonial shields further expands one's appreciation.

Beginning collectors are often tempted to buy everything in sight. The lure of the great availability and variety even within the 25¢ to $10 budget, is almost irresistible. Eventually, of course, space limitations, common sense, and personal tastes and interests help to sift and refine choices.

Specialties can be narrow or broad: Within the folk art category there is scope for Indian examples (Maine is a good browsing and shopping state for the Indian basket collector), Appalachian, or sweet grass baskets. This last category is often erroneously referred to as Gullah basketry, Gullah being the dialect of these South Carolina basketmakers whose craft represents one of the few directly descended from Africa which has been produced steadily since the eighteenth century. The sweet grass basketmakers still ply their wares directly to the buyers along U.S. Highway 17, north of Charleston and Mt. Pleasant.

Antique baskets are harder and more expensive to come by than new ones, which, while made traditionally, often incorporate shapes and functions appealing to current lifestyles. Both domestic and foreign folk art baskets can be obtained in sales outlets set up through state arts commissions, crafts guilds, supply and/or crafts galleries, or collected during one's travels (Chapter 5).

Modern artists creating baskets often use yarns rather than natural grasses and reeds. Many combine techniques or introduce nontradi-

This sampling of baskets from around the globe, ranging in price from $3 to $60, was photographed at the Niddy Noddy in Croton-on-Hudson, New York.

Bottom step: A group of eleven double-plaited and leather coiled bridal baskets from Africa, each made to fit inside the other. It is said that when a bride has demonstrated her proficiency in basketmaking with a "set" such as this, she is ready to marry. The basket at the right is an inexpensive wall basket from Korea.

Middle step: A lidded, coiled milk container from Africa, and an American Indian twined basket (old).

Top step: Appalachian baskets have become increasingly sought after in recent years. This one was made by Mary Helton of Virginia who has been making baskets for most of her seventy years.

Prospective buyers examine low country South Carolina sweet grass baskets at the stand of basketmaker Mary Jane Bennett who is weaving a large "show" basket. Her stand is one of more than forty scattered for several miles along U.S. Highway 17, north of Charleston. The baskets are for sale the year round, Monday through Saturday, and range in price from $5 to $50. Photo courtesy South Carolina Arts Commission.

Sharon La Pierre's baskets are double collectibles, a chance for gourd aficionados to introduce some fibers into their collection and for basketry buffs to enjoy the natural beauty of gourds. The coiling method and use of feathers are traditional to basketry.

tional methods. Here, as with all new art, bargains are possible for those willing to trust their taste and instinct, and by seeking out unknown talent at small shops and local fairs rather than at the more prestigious outlets. Those inclined to intersperse their collecting with some of their own handwork can enroll in a proliferating range of workshops. There are also books from which one can learn to do and to collect, or both.

Fabric Dolls

The doll is probably one of *the* major collectibles throughout the world. However, the fabric doll, at least in its traditional rag doll image, has for the most part been the exception, if status achieved in terms of monetary value is to be used as any kind of yardstick. Nevertheless, once again the energizing effects of the handcrafts movement coupled with the interest in anything considered to be folk art has given stature to all types of fabric dolls and given fabric dollmakers new impetus to practice professionally what they have always loved doing.

In 1970 Jean Ray Laury, a California fabric designer and writer and inveterate dollmaker herself, wrote a book reflecting a growing interest in the fabric doll as art as well as craft. Since then the traditional fabric doll, along with knitted and woven ones, has found many new and avid collectors. Some very distinctly 1960s–1970s dolls emerged, with the big ingredients of this period being polyester fiber, discarded pantyhose, and nylon stockings. These pantyhose dolls, as they have come to be called, lend themselves to wonderful characterizations and can be and are being made in all sizes. Sometimes the heads alone are used as part of other art, as in Joan Schulze's wonderful bicentennial quilt, which uses pantyhose doll heads as the star centers of her flag design. Other dollmakers have gone beyond the simple, cuddly object to create life-sized forms of hardened fabrics. These have found favor with serious collectors, not of dolls but of sculptures, for that is exactly what these life studies are.

All contemporary dolls, whether small and simple toys, traditional or ultramodern, involve the maker as well as the final owner in collecting. For the creator, collecting means scouring her attic, antique shops, flea markets, and house sales for the proper costuming details. The buyer in turn collects her dolls at fairs, folk festivals, or shops. The "beyond doll" sculptures are available through art galleries or directly from artists in their studios. Prices are obviously at extremes of the bottom and top.

Another interesting doll collectible is the stuff-and-sew doll—animal or human characters painted or otherwise imprinted on fabric and then stuffed and sewed by the doll owner. There are many silk-screened reproductions of genuinely antique versions. Some are avail-

Detail of Joan Schulze's bicentennial flag quilt, showing stocking doll heads used as star centers. Photo, Chuck Koehler.

The dolls of childhood are often the start of it all, both for the dollmaker and the collector. Here we see Ithaca doll artist Liese Bronfenbrenner with mementos of her childhood: A metal mesh doll crib and dolls, circa 1920. The boy has composition arms and a bisque head; the girl doll is celluloid. The little straw suitcase and accessories are from the same era.

Nesting dolls usually bring to mind the wooden ones made in Poland. Here is the nesting theme interpreted by Liese for the textile enthusiast. The Matroyska Peasant Girls range in size from two inches for the tiniest of the five, to fourteen inches.

For the atypical doll collector, here is a family group with molded faces and bike appliquéd to padded muslin. This type of very personalized textile collectible is of course only possible when buying from living artists, many of whom enjoy the challenge of commemorating family celebrations.

I have two family portraits (one of Mike and me and one of our son and daughter) woven by Mary Lou Higgins of Erie, Pennsylvania, and a more abstract batik painting of our interests as well as of us by Shirley Venit Anger of Brooklyn. One of these days I hope to add one of Liese's wonderful doll portraits to this textile family album.

The use of fabric hardened like papier mâché gives Kay Ritter's larger-than-life figures sculptural solidity, without losing the fabric's tactile draped and wrinkled appearance. Kay's prodigious scouring of flea markets for old clothes, shoes, bags, bits of lace, and whatever is needed to give her people character defies classification as anything other than wonderful.

Knitted dolls, especially those from South America, are collectors' favorites. I've discovered several charming ones in antique shops and at street fairs, some old, most fairly recent. This little gem, notable for its coin appliqués, was photographed at Putumayo Gallery in New York City.

Some might quarrel with including animal forms within a doll-collecting chapter, but then Kari Lonning's woven beasts are collected by people such as actress Julie Christie, not so much as dolls or toy animals or even sculptures, but as imposing personalities in fiber.

able in miniature or in finger-puppet versions, and a group of these adds up to a nice shelf collection.

Those with little or no interest in dolls (and there are some who don't share what at times seems the whole world's doll mania) but who do love clothing and accessories, might consider doll clothes as a way of collecting miniature costumes. This type of collection has the advantage of being portable, easy to display in a small space, though with both dolls and miniatures so tremendously popular, don't expect small in size to equal small in price.

Potpourri

As already stated at the outset, a book with as broad and open-ended an approach as this one can only lead the reader to the threshold of some of the most likely possibilities. Choices for inclusion were based on popularity, availability in a wide price range, and potential for diversification within and beyond the suggested category. Some things worth considering eluded classification into specific chapters. This seemed insufficient if downright silly grounds for omission and so this potpourri, ranging from what some regard as a sublime example of the tapestry in miniature, the Stephengraph, to some not-so-ridiculous suggestions for establishing your own category of some-day-to-be-valuables, plus some stimulating ideas for what I like to call mixed-media collecting.

WOVEN SILK PICTURES

With all Victoriana rapidly approaching the "hot" collectible stage, Stevengraphs and other types of silk pictures, ribbons, and bookmarks are likely to enjoy a fresh wave of collecting enthusiasm.

To the true-blue Stevengraph collectors, and there are enough of these to have sustained an association of some two hundred members for over a decade, the myriad woven silk products emanating from Coventry, England, between 1860 and the first decade of this century should *not* be automatically or generically identified as Stevengraphs. Collectors reserve this term for pictures made by the man after whom they are named, Thomas Stevens, mounted and matted for framing. It was Stevens who adapted the Jacquard loom to accommodate the width of the pictures. Stevengraphs from his factory can be identified by the lettering *woven in silk* (for the earliest and most desirable ones), or *woven in silk by Thomas Stevens inventor and manufacturer*. Some without this lettering from the Stevens factory's last production run of pictures represent the Stevengraph's authentic "last hurrah."

While the mounted Stevengraphs with the aforementioned lettered

WOVEN IN PURE SILK.

Signing of the Declaration of Independence

JULY 4TH, 1776.

Authentic Stevengraph pictures are mounted, and stamped on the matte are the words "Woven in pure silk," as in this example from the collection of Lewis Smith, president and founder of the Stevengraph Collectors' Association, Irvington-on-Hudson, New York.

provenances are the ones which attract the investment-minded collector, having fetched very respectable auction bids (mostly at London auctions), there are enough stories of fine examples found in antique and junkshops to encourage the bargain hunter. What's more, if your own personal esthetics more than potential value dictates your collecting, you can stretch both your dollars and your chances of finding interesting items by considering unmounted Stevengraphs, the less popular subjects, and the pictures woven by the numerous and frequently quite successful imitators. Woven ribbons, valentines, and bookmarks can further widen your collecting range.

SOME-DAY-TO-BE-VALUABLES

Is is interesting to note that upon the woven picture's decline in popularity the Stevens factory converted to the production of woven ribbons for sailors' uniforms. These were at that time considered even less likely to be of interest to collectors than the bookmarks and pictures were when first brought onto the market. Yet, a number of knowledgeable textile collectors have stressed the potential value of and interest in woven and machine-embroidered clothing tags. I would personally add to this some of the more interesting embroidered decorative sew-on patches. My daughter started such a collection quite by accident at age six when someone burnt a cigarette hole into her first and brand-new ski jacket. We decided to buy her one of the patches sold at the ski shop to sew over the offending hole—little

*One never knows what will be
valuable. Machine-made lace nice
and mellowed with several
decades of age is still available
in large, perfect-condition pieces
and samplerlike rolls, at very
reasonable prices. The labels are
from Joellen Sommer's gradually
accumulated collection of
embroidered ski resort labels.*

realizing that in the long run a new jacket might have been cheaper. You see, that patch led to another at every ski resort we visited over the next ten years, not only for her but also for her brother. For awhile we kept transferring patches to larger jackets, but eventually Joellen carefully removed and saved all the patches and mounted most of them onto a backing fabric as a memory hanging. She used Velcro backings so the labels can be removed and, if desired, used on clothing once again. Others whom I've interviewed cite not only machine-embroidered clothing labels, especially those made of silk, as potentially valuable, but also machine-made lace, particularly from the 1920s and 1930s.

Lest you think some of these suggestions for potentially valuable textile collecting are perhaps a bit farfetched, here are some excerpts from an annotated list of over thirty items sent in by Otto Thieme. Otto is a professional textile researcher and artist whose collection includes several coverlets made by John Schneider (see page 36) and the outstanding and rare seventeenth-century English beaded picture illustrated on the cover, so his recommendations are not to be taken lightly. The items are listed at random, and are not in any particular order of importance:

- Crochet samplers
- Twentieth-century needlepoint
- Berlin woolwork
- Nineteenth-century handwoven fabric, not coverlets but sheets, shirts, towels, and fragments
- Bicentennial items—which Otto feels will turn up in rummage sales
- First Communion hankies (see pages 45–46 on hankies in general)

- Bras, girdles, slips, panties—Otto thinks a collection of these might be exceedingly valuable in seventy years
- Anything by "Vera"
- Designer sheets (Author's Note: And don't forget designer scarves)
- "Lace" curtains
- Pure silk ties and those owned by members of a family (see Ron Spark's collection described earlier)
- Handmade baby clothing
- Potholders—The Center for the History of American Needlework agrees with Otto on this, having mounted a traveling exhibit of "kitchen needlework" (see Chapter 7)
- Shoelaces—about which Otto says "you'd never believe!" ... though we do believe and refer readers to page 102
- Campaign ribbons
- Anything with a picture of Jesus on it
- Embroidered handbags
- Pincushions
- Iron-on embroidery patterns
- Carpet swatches
- Any type of fabric with flowers
- Printed calendar towels
- Imported or ethnic textiles (see Chapter 5)
- Cottons imported from India
- Artist/craftsman textiles—Otto suggests as we have in various places in this book that readers take advantage of the opportunities for discovering "unknowns" and having special designs and themes commissioned.

Tips for Making Current Fabrics Historically Valuable

In addition to his very extensive list of Some-Day-to-Be-Valuables that readers might consider, Otto sent the following suggestions for those interested in turning currently bought yardage into a collection of historic significance:

Purchase at least one full repeat of a print.

Record all information on the bolt end, as well as the name of the store, the price, and the date of purchase. In addition, keep a record of the measurements, fabrication techniques, fiber content and analysis (including color, spin, ply, thread count, etc.). For the true historian-collector, Otto further suggests a written record by the collector on these topics: How the design "fits" its time, something obvious now but not in ten years; any publicity concerning the fabric or its design; any information on the manufacturer, distributor, or merchant which helps researchers to date fabrics; how well a particular fabric has sold, along with any other information to be gleaned from salespersons.

Fabrics and fibers combine very handsomely with other types of furnishings. Quite often some aspect of a nontextile item will suggest ways of using stockpiled textile scraps. This is a particularly fruitful area for those who like to add their own skills and talents to their collections. I know no one who better exemplifies the simplicity and variety of mixed-media collecting than Nancy Lipe. Some of her Victorian costumes with her own needlework touches were shown earlier. In the following illustrations, we see the excitement that even a little fiber can add to everything from hatracks to lamps and framed stamp and butterfly collections.

Here crochet is worked in a free-form pattern suggested by the elongated moth pattern of the lamp. The fiber addition also serves to hide the chain needed to electrify the old lamp.

The circular pattern of this Victorian loveseat's Venus pattern, with its long seaweedlike hair flowing across the back, inspired a bunch of pillows with concentrically crocheted circle designs. Some have small ball fringes to echo the small ball-like protrusions in the wood and the fish eyes in the gargoyle arms. These are the same kind of circles Nancy Lipe crocheted to recycle a thrift-shop bathrobe into a coat for daughter Miae (see section on old clothes).

This lamp, not quite old enough to be Victorian but of personal importance because it was used during Nancy Lipe's birth, is covered with glued-on fabric puffs like those from the 1920s yo-yo quilts. If you can't find such a quilt in poor enough condition to cut apart, you can always make your own puffs by basting and shirring fabric circles or, as in the illustration, squares.

Here we have a four-way collection: Stamps, butterflies, a Victorian frame, plus two hand-crocheted butterflies. You might find embroidered or tatted ready-made butterflies in bins of discarded old needlework and notions stores's supplies.

Old Victorian hatracks often call for some special decorative touches. Here, a quickly-made spider web, complete with silk button and thread-covered wire.

5.
For the Traveling Textile Enthusiast

There isn't a place on the entire globe where you are not likely to find some fascinating additions for your textile collection, whether your interests and budget tend toward small pieces of wearable folk art or large tapestries by well-known weavers. Many a collection has actually been launched during a vacation, and built up via follow-up trips. In some instances, traveling and collecting become so all-consuming that the collector turns dealer-importer, thus quite literally having her collecting cake and cashing in on it too. To take this a step further, these importers in turn make it possible for those who by choice or necessity remain close to home to become armchair collectors.

Not all collecting requires a passport. I have already cited the Navajo rugs sold at auction in New Mexico and the sweet grass baskets sold near Mt. Pleasant, South Carolina, by basketmakers who still speak the Gullah dialect and work in the tradition of their West African forebears. A very busy domestic itinerary can be planned around the ever-increasing number of special gallery and museum exhibits, regularly scheduled antique and crafts shows and flea markets. Finally, whether you travel abroad or domestically, there are many fine permanent textile collections which, though not a source for acquisition, *are* a rich wellspring for learning more about your subject.

In order to keep this discussion within manageable confines, I will highlight some collectibles which hold great appeal to sophisticated as well as amateur collectors, and which oftentimes can be bought without actually going to the source of their production. Neither inclusion nor omission of certain countries or types of textiles should be regarded as judgmental on my part. What's more, in spite of the oft-voiced gloomy comments from old-time collectors about the really good things being "gone forever," much remains to be discovered for those with a sharp eye and a spirit of adventure. Who's to say that once the influence of industrialization and tourism is absorbed into some of the ancient cultures that new and different expressions of creative endeavor will not result? Some of the charming designs to be found in modern versions of my first detailed collectible, the mola, are a case in point.

Molas

The intricately layered and stitched mola panels made by the Cuna Indian women of the San Blas Islands off the coast of Panama are only about a hundred and twenty-five years old, though they trace their origins to the brightly colored body paintings of the sixteenth century and the transference of these paintings to fabric during the 1800s.

While importers usually sell molas as separate panels, they are actually made as the front and back for blouses worn by the Cuna women since the Victorian era. The mola's status as genuine folk art is a fairly recent phenomenon and collecting interest shows no sign of waning, especially with a growing number of seriously reviewed art exhibits both in the United States and in Europe.

Just what are the techniques and design elements which make the molas unique? Like the pieced patchwork quilt, it epitomizes ingenuity in transforming one type of fabric into a newly designed one. The mola design evolves not from small pieces but by layering two or more contrasting sections of cotton on top of one another, then snipping through the layer to create design images. The raw fabric edges are sewn down to the next layer with very fine stitches. Although the technique is different, molas, like patchwork quilts, often present very striking op-art effects. Another comparison may be drawn from the fact that just as early patchworkers would pass on favorite patterns to friends and relatives even as they created their own designs, so the Cuna women share certain designs but also draw on everything in their environment for others. This incorporation of visual images and symbols from the surroundings has resulted in some fascinating blends of old and new traditionally made molas, with trademarks from advertisements intermingling with the Cunas' own religious and historic sources.

Who are the collectors who have contributed to the mola's meteoric rise? Jane Gehring, for many years a teacher of textile printing at the University of Oregon and herself a textile artist, is typical. She was an early collector and of the many interesting examples she owns the one she likes best is the one she has dubbed "Mary Had a Little Lamb" since it was so obviously copied from a coloring or nursery rhyme book.

Barbara Simon and daughter Jennifer look over some of the molas personally selected in the course of two trips to the San Blas Islands. All have extensive and fine hand stitchery details, with thread always matching the color of the fabrics. Frames for the molas were designed and constructed by Dr. Simon.

Just as typical are Barbara and Dan Simon of Port Washington, New York. The Simons had accumulated various small objects—some painted gourds, jewelry, wooden objects—but it was a visit to San Blas that turned them into collectors on a bigger scale. The molas bought on their first trip were not impulse purchases. Barbara had heard about them, taken time to read up on both the art and the people creating it and so had some guidelines to go with her inherently good taste to help differentiate between the poor "tourist" mola and the more genuine article. She feels they were especially lucky on their first outing in finding a guide who took them to less traveled parts of San Blas, and in getting there at the end of a festival when all the people had been celebrating and were inclined to sell things not normally for sale. That first buying trip led to a return visit, this time with daughter Jennifer who invested in her own special collection of small molas which she plans one day to appliqué to some clothing.

Are good molas still available?

Some of the truly awful ersatz molas being sold both in Panama and in gift shops tend to hide the gems beneath the rubbish, but if you are discriminating you can still find many worth having. This is true even of import and museum gift shops, which are dependent

The Simons bought all except Jennifer's small molas in their authentic original forms, which means that every purchase yields two panels. Since the Cuna people are very small, it is unlikely that the original blouses can actually be worn. Many people do appliqué the panels to other clothing as pockets, upper arm panels, blouse bodices, or they make them into pillows and bags.

upon the antique store's equivalent of the "picker," making their stock only as good as their suppliers. Here are some guidelines:

1. Look for hand-stitching with matching thread.
2. The finer the detail, the finer the mola. It is an interesting sidelight that the finest detailing is found in the molas of the 1950s and 1960s, rather than the really old ones.
3. Watch out for cheap shortcut additions—i.e., machine-appliquéd rickrack to feign layered designs.
4. Importers carrying molas still attached to the original blouse are likely to have a better quality supply.

Tapas

True tapa cloth is made by steeping and beating the inner bark of a mulberry tree, with designs usually printed with stencils and dabbers. Tapas have not enjoyed the widespread popularity of molas, though they have been used by the Polynesians, Japanese, Sumatrans, and Melanesians. Jane Gehring, who collects both tapas and molas, feels the former will enjoy increasing interest as part of the revival in kindred ancient methods of making paper and felt.

Like many old crafts, tapa making has been in danger of disappearing. Jane Gehring tells of a Samoan woman who expressed doubts about the tapa's future when Jane bought some of her first tapas back in 1967. However, when Jane returned in 1975, the same woman had managed to interest her daughters and other village women in learning and had also begun to lecture and demonstrate to tourists.

Many people unfamiliar with authentic tapas buy souvenir products, unaware that a huge tapa can still be bought in the neighborhood of $30. As Jane says, "the tapas are inexpensive—it's getting there that's costly." For those wishing to study tapas from all the different areas in the South Pacific, the Bishop Museum in Honolulu probably offers the most extensive representation.

African Textiles

African art in all its varied forms has long been recognized for its vitalization of the work of such artists as Picasso and Klee. Batiks, appliqué embroidery, woven raffia cloth, and baskets (see the nested bridal baskets and milk container on page 72) have been and are avidly studied and collected. Thelma Newman, in her beautiful and scholarly book, *Contemporary African Arts and Crafts,* echoes my own previously voiced feeling that the concern about the influence of foreign buyers may be overly pessimistic. "Why should people of a country

The brilliant appliqués from Dahomey are said to have originated on raffia cloth, before European trade cloth came into common usage in 1890. In picking the best among the many small hangings and pillows of this type available, the collector might do well to keep this large hanging photographed at the Niddy Noddy in Croton-on-Hudson in mind as a yardstick. It is a particularly fine and rare example, with each square identifying a different king and the year he reigned.

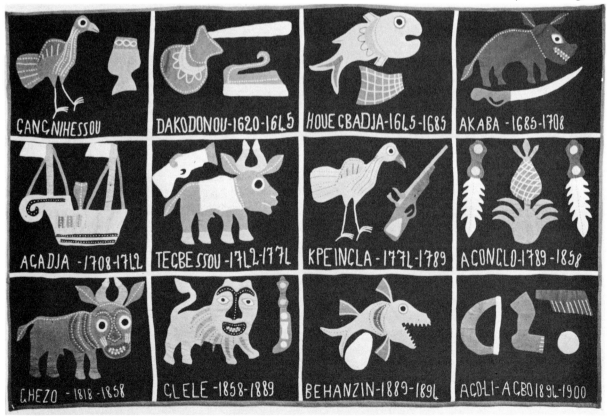

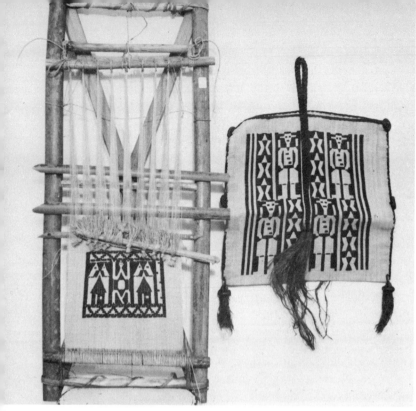

The African raffia loom is very similar in design to the Navajo Indian loom. It is used to make small mats and bags like the one at right used by the Bamileke people of Cameroon for hunting in the forest. Photographed at the Niddy-Noddy.

not flow and move with the times?" she asks. She admits that some traditions are indeed gone but sees no real loss of vitality in the African artist's "responding to new styles, new clients, and new functions." This does not mean of course that the new collector need not be forewarned of the more shoddy adaptations and be able to circumvent them by learning as much as possible through studying museum collections and visiting African art galleries.

Functional Tapestries and Embroideries for Inexpensive, International Collecting

Baskets and bags have already been discussed as overall types of collectibles. The traveling textile enthusiast can add to an existing collection in either category. He or she can collect with an eye to circling the globe or concentrate on examples from a particular culture.

If I were hard-pressed to single out one particular item in this area worth the special attention of the low-budget collector, it would probably be the small coca bags woven in the Bolivian Highlands and in Cuzco, Peru, and used by the men to carry coca leaves which are chewed to alleviate hunger and cold. Handwoven on Inca looms in sheep's wool, llama, and alpaca, these handsome little bags offer all the design and color intricacies of larger textile weavings on a miniature and affordable scale. Most are less than $20. As yet, they are not as ubiquitous to the import and museum shop scene as some other

*For the Traveling
Textile Enthusiast*

*Two functional tapestries from different parts
of the world, photographed at the Niddy Noddy.
The large Persian spindle bag at left is the
type once used by Nomadic weavers to carry all
their supplies. Small coca bags, like the one at
the right, come in a variety of designs and afford
a fine opportunity for collecting highly portable
and affordable miniature tapestries.*

items and a number of import sellers whom I asked seemed unfamiliar
with them. I did see some handsome examples both at Irene Miller's
Niddy Noddy at Croton-on-Hudson, New York, and at Dan Storper's
Putumayo gallery on Lexington Avenue, New York City. Larger and
more expensive are the Persian spindle bags ($40 to $100 seemed an
average range) woven by nomads to hold their weaving materials.
With nomadic lifestyles becoming increasingly obsolete, these are well
worth buying while they can be bought.

In the basket category I've seen the Ecuadorian knotless netted
container gain in status in the past two or three years. Those actively
involved in fiber crafts recognize its construction as being more akin

*For the knotless netted container collector, finding new and different design patterns is a real challenge.
Using the ceiling as a display space is a great idea for all kinds of collections, as illustrated in this
photograph taken at Putumayo Gallery in New York City.*

to needlework than to the traditional basketry techniques of coiling and twining. Knotless netting is in fact a buttonhole stitch worked independently, rather than as a fabric embroidery stitch. All the examples of recycling in this book employ either this knotless netting, buttonhole stitching, or basic crochet. The designs of the Ecuadorian containers are created by changing or carrying extra colors, as in tapestry knitting or crocheting. The collector will soon see that while the containers are available in many stores, the more distinctive designs require some special searching.

Clothing from Other Cultures

Clothing, like bags and baskets, can be collected on an international scale. Sometimes a collector buys clothing to convert into something else (i.e., mola blouses into hangings), or nonclothing items are refashioned. Some garments from other cultures can be worn as is, giving their new owners a special sense of being in physical touch with two worlds. Both Cathy Parenti and Yvonne Porcella collect all manner of textile fabrics and accessories for inspiration and/or recycling. Both own and wear elaborate ethnic dresses.

Cathy Parenti is a native of Brooklyn, New York. She always dreamed of going to Afghanistan, and ten years ago she did. Her

Cathy Parenti and Sedig Malikyar wearing and surrounded by some of their Afghanistan treasures. Her Koochee dress is a very rare one, heavy with coins, buttons, and jewels. Sedig's ikat coat, while very regal-looking, is worn by ordinary men. Cathy has transformed some of these coats into skirts and vests. The hanging in back of Cathy is a patchwork, known as a karakeb in Afghanistan.

More international collectibles for bag people. The two bags at right are from an Indian Sari sash, the other items are all Afghanistan and made to be used as purses. The small drawstring bag near the sari sash is somewhat reminiscent of the Victorian miser's purse and everything you see can be bought in the $10 neighborhood. From the collection of Cathy Parenti and Sedig Malikyar.

Yvonne Porcella wearing one of her California-collected Bedouin dresses, with another on the wall in back of her. She is lecturing on the inspiration she derives from ethnic textiles she has collected. In her right hand she holds a Jacquard-patterned knitted sock from Bavaria and in the left a glove it inspired.

love affair with the country started her buying fabrics, hangings, and clothing and eventually her collection became so big that she became a dealer. Today she has a partner, Sedig Malikyar, who enables her to spend some time in Brooklyn as well as in Afghanistan. The nomadic or Koochee dress she is wearing in the picture with Sedig is one of a whole collection.

Yvonne Porcella might have bought her Bedouin wedding dress, circa 1928, from a collector-importer like Cathy if they lived in the same state. Everything Yvonne has collected—ethnic garments, belts, bags, hangings—has been accumulated without her ever leaving the country, or for that matter her native state of California. Yvonne's collection is also the basis for professional involvement. However, instead of selling her extras, she uses both the things she makes and those she buys as the basis for lectures and classes, showing the correlation between contemporary and ethnic fiber work.

Naïve Textile "Paintings"

The unstudied simplicity and directness of folk art stitchery paintings make them popular collectibles. The yarn paintings of Mexico and

#5-12

The brightness and charm of these stitchery paintings from Panama blend well with Barbara and Dan Simon's larger mola collection.

An example of Chile's political appliqué paintings from the private collection of Dan Storper. Dan feels his childhood fondness for the illustrations in the Dr. Doolittle books influenced his interest in South American textile art.

Panama have been enjoyed by low-budget collectors for some time. For those who lean toward message art, a very interesting group of appliqué paintings have been newly created since the ascent of the Chilean Junta. Working-class Chilean women whose husbands have disappeared have stitched appliqué pictures depicting the world they live in—filled with the contrasts between rich and poor, powerful and powerless. The appliqués vary in size and sophistication and have been cooperatively marketed to help these women sustain themselves and also tell their stories.

6.
Corollaries

Just as the woodworker needs a lathe and a toolbox, lumber and nails, so the needleworker and weaver need pins, needles, work containers, thimbles, shuttles, looms, spindles, and, of course, yarn and thread. Some of these were previewed in my illustrated interview with Bucky King in Chapter 2. What follows is a further elaboration on the corollary theme.

Textile Tools and Materials

Most tool collectors don't start out as such. Instead, they are actively involved doers and what they buy is what they use. Before long, however, many become attuned to the variety and beauty of some of the items they need and so they cross the bridge that separates the buyer of necessities from the collector. I guess I'm my own best example of how this works: When I was preparing my first fiber crafts book, *A New Look at Crochet*, I owned the standard variety of store-bought aluminum hooks. As I researched the history of the craft, I came across illustrations and examples of hooks carved out of wood and ivory. By the time the book project was done I had "rewarded" myself with some hand-turned and carved wooden hooks as well as one made from hardened seaweed! Some of these can be seen in the crochet how-to photograph on page 120. Of course, once you have wooden and seaweed hooks, you've also got to have one made from ivory . . . and so it goes. I guess it should also come as no surprise that from the moment I completed my companion to the crochet book, *A New Look at Knitting*, I began to keep a weather eye out for an interesting set of knitting needles. When we photographed some of the many

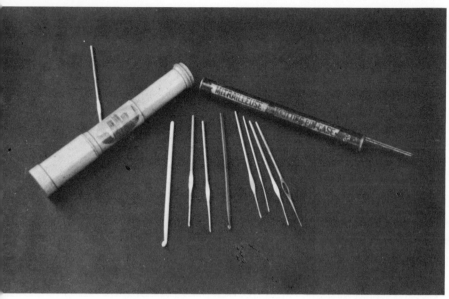

Old wood, metal, and ivory crochet hooks and two containers for steel knitting pins. The one at right is a metal container with swivel-top opening for four sets of pins which became part of the author's collection during this photo session at the Niddy Noddy.

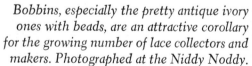

Bobbins, especially the pretty antique ivory ones with beads, are an attractive corollary for the growing number of lace collectors and makers. Photographed at the Niddy Noddy.

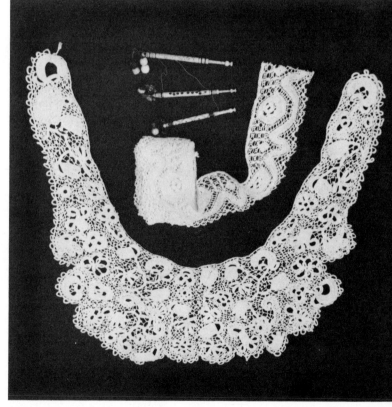

goodies to be found at Irene Miller's Niddy Noddy, I saw exactly what I'd been looking for: an English-made tubular metal case with an ingenious top which twisted, like a grated cheese container, to four different openings, each of which held a different set of double-pointed fine steel knitting pins.

Other small tools considered highly collectible are bobbins used for making bobbin lace, bodkins used to punch out fabric as in Richelieu-type embroidery, tatting shuttles, and thread-cutting devices.

SEWING BIRDS

Sewing birds were once a much-used accessory. The bird functioned as an extra hand, especially for sewing hems on long ruffles and rib-

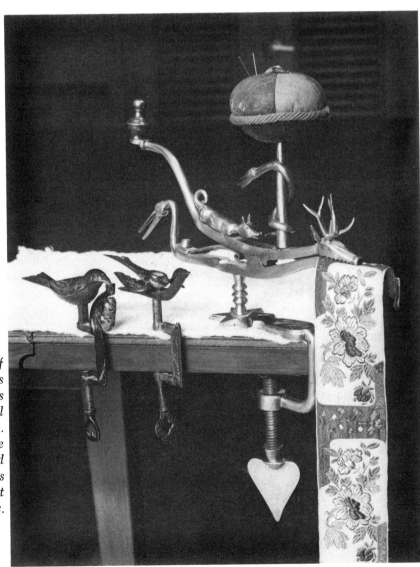

Phalice Ayers assembled some of her prized treasures for this photo. The little bird at left is complete with its original pincushion to match the handle. The one at right did not fare as well. The very elaborate bird holds a piece of silk ribbon in its mouth, as it did when it first entered its owner's life.

bons. Some came with their own pincushions, though these are often
lost or worn out on old and much-used implements. There are simple
and elaborate birds, new ones as well as old ones. The new ones lack
the mystery and antique value, but I've seen some very attractive
modern versions which are sure to age well.

THIMBLES

The thimble is in a class of its own, an established *super* collectible.
Collectors number in the hundreds of thousands, and have their own
organization and a newsletter (*The Collector's Circle Gazette*) published by Roz Belford. Her very successful mail-order sewing supply
and thimble company was literally pulled out of a thimble—lots of
thimbles really, since Roz herself has been collecting all her life.

What accounts for the enormous popularity of this tiny sewing
aid? To start with, its size. As pointed out previously, the near-mania
surrounding all things miniature has proven that the smallest and not
the biggest is likely to be considered the best. Being small, the thimble
is easily transported from one place to another, can be collected on

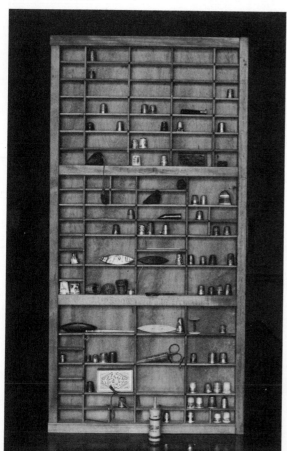

*Finding a proper showcase for one's thimbles and
related treasures is half the fun of collecting. For
Phalice Ayers this proved to be an old printer's type
case. It holds thimbles from all around the world in
silver, gold, brass, ivory, tin, porcelain, leather, and
heavy fabric. The group in the lower right-hand section
consists of advertising thimbles. For visual variety,
there's scissors, shuttle, tiny ivory thread holder,
and a silver-topped needle sharpener.*

trips without worrying about how to get home, and of course is easily displayed in even the tightest living space.

The thimble's popularity can also be measured by its availability and variety. From the Stone Age on, finger protectors were made in every conceivable kind of material including leather, wood, stone, ivory, porcelain, bronze, and other metals. Since its usage has been so widespread, the thimble has long been considered the kind of souvenir commemorative or advertising item that would appeal to a wide audience. Thus, there are plenty of choices ranging from the ordinary to the extraordinary.

Last but by no means least in accounting for the thimble's status as a "serious" collectible is its intrinsic value and this undoubtedly accounts for the high priority most collectors give to silver and gold thimbles. As with any fine metal object, there are hallmarks to check, trademarks, and other marks to learn about, plus all the other intricacies that are part of collecting for value as well as pleasure. Needless to say, thimbles need not be costly and valuable to be enjoyed. Most of Phalice Ayer's thimbles are in the $5 to $10 price category and her all-time best buy is a carved ivory thimble obtained for five cents because it had a crack!

Needlework Cases, Boxes, and Tables

In medieval times when pins were extremely precious, women wore needlecases attached to their girdles. As the scope of needlework

Phalice Ayers owns an Oriental lacquer sewing table, circa 1900, in which she keeps her most meaningful possessions: For example, her great-grandmother's glasses, a bobbin, darning helper, two fitted cases, and a crochet hook and a pair of knitting needles which started "life" as molding in a railroad car. A train was derailed while crossing the Farmington River in Connecticut during a bad blizzard long ago. Many people were killed and pieces of the molding were scattered in the nearby fields. An ingenious uncle of Phalice's, upon finding some of this wood, made knitting needles and a crochet hook for his mother to use in making clothes for her five children. And so from tragedy in Connecticut, to treasure in Spokane, Washington. Note the wonderful macramé fringe.

increased the small cases grew into larger bags which were eventually followed by needlework boxes. The needlework table is yet another extension and enlargement of the box and both box and table are regarded with great esteem by all who collect antique furnishings. During Victorian days, when both sewing and writing boxes were much in vogue, it was not uncommon to find a table with dual functions.

The sewing table is usually collected as a one-of-a-kind piece of furniture rather than in any quantity. Many women who have revived decoupage as a fine craft, in the tradition of the Venetian furniture-makers of the sixteenth and seventeenth centuries, have refinished old sewing boxes and tables, or worked on contemporary raw wood reproductions. These contemporary pieces are very much heirlooms of the future.

WEAVING AND SPINNING TOOLS

Like needlework tools, the weaver's tools hold great fascination for the ingenuity reflected in some of the devices, their antiquity, and their esthetic appeal. Spinning wheels have been used as "interesting"

In Chapter 4 there's a section called The Best of Both Worlds in which artists who incorporate antique needlework into contemporary hangings are discussed. This concept is not limited to hangings. To wit, this unusual, contemporary knitting needle case (can you see the knitting needles?) which give new life and meaning to an obsolete Singer Sewing machine part. Artist Norma Minkowitz's knack for making distinctly new statements using traditional knitting techniques have made her a favorite with fiber art collectors everywhere. Photo Kobler/Dyer Studios.

In colonial times, spinning wheels and looms for weaving narrow bands were considered ordinary household equipment. This tape loom and wheel were one of several seen at Rock Hall, Lawrence, New York.

accessories for homes where no one spins. Some people transform them into tables and lamps and this is all right, I suppose, though I enjoy seeing them in a home where their presence makes a meaningful connection with the lifestyles and interests of the owners. The items to be collected are marvelously diverse and can be collected from many different places, domestic and foreign.

The subject of collecting materials is primarily a matter for the doer-collector and even then, most who weave or knit or crochet don't think of themselves as collectors. Yet, unless you're strictly an Orlon and acrylic, follow-the-pattern project maker you will find yourself searching out interesting and unusual materials in order to stimulate interesting and unusual designs.

Hanks of brightly dyed yarn suspended from a ceiling, spools stacked onto shelves, etc., are so decorative that they could exist in their own right. Usually they don't stay in their fiber state for long, though they don't really disappear but simply reappear in another and even more enjoyable form. The excitement and danger of being bitten by the yarn-collecting bug as part of traveling was well described by weaver Nell Znamierowski in an article entitled "Odyssey of Yarn" (May–June 1969, *Craft Horizons*): "Collecting yarns can be a global preoccupation. I've touched only a few in comparison to what there is to see—one can go on and on until it becomes pointless to return home again, since home has turned into one large yarn warehouse."

To many, like myself, being able to apply traditional techniques to materials not intended as yarn at all is part of the fun of collecting one's materials from flea markets and job-lot sales rather than from conventional yarn stores. Ribbons by the roll, fabric cut into strips, piping from upholstery, all are great finds. I bought my large spool of shoelacing at a flea market even before I heard Otto Thieme's prediction about shoelaces as some-day-to-be-valuables. I thought this would be a nice contemporary material for making a giant-sized version of a once popular type of knitted pincushion. My pincushion really got away from me and became a sculpture, but then that's what makes collecting rather than buying materials so interesting.

Books, Magazines, and Other Paper Memorabilia

If you buy just a small fraction of the books available on the many phases of textiles, you are well on the way toward owning a fine collection. If you're a novice, you'll be amazed at the number of books, booklets, magazines, and newsletters published and being published. Weaving alone can comprise a sizable collection which in turn could be subdivided into historical surveys and how-to technique books. As more and more new books are published, older ones disappear from store shelves, to be found mostly in libraries, second-hand shops and from textile book specialists, and this is the stuff that old book collections are made of.

Most who buy books, like those who buy tools, do so more for the sake of active reference than for the sake of collecting them in their

A large spool of shoe lacing bought at a flea market was used to make a seat-sized cushion similar to once-popular pincushions. The technique is basic knitting: Large sized knitting needles are used to make a long, narrow strip of fabric which is seamed and stuffed with polyester, and then coiled.

Before stitching my coil into a permanent cushion form, I decided to manipulate it into a sculptural form. I like it so much sitting on top of one of my first pieces of needlecraft furniture, a commercial spool chest, that it never did make it into a pillow. The book contains all the copies of Godey's Lady's Book for 1874, a magazine worth a chapter of its own.

own right. However, as the bookshelves fill up and the pleasure in what is owned deepens, many get into the concept of owning everything available at least in one particular interest. Even if you don't buy books for their potential as collectibles now, you can do a few things to give yourself the option of changing your mind:

1. Buy the first edition of the book. Many will have the words *First Edition* printed on the page containing the copyright date. If a book has had several printings, that history will be recorded on the same page and means you are *not* buying a first edition.
2. Take a cue from Otto Thieme's advice about making fabrics historically valuable and attach a little pocket to the back of the book, or keep a separate file, in which you keep information such as where you bought the book and when. You might include clippings of ads and reviews or writeups about the author.
3. Try to buy books autographed by the author. Some bookstores carry a certain number of autographed books for those unable to make personal contact.
4. Old books often have interesting bits of data from previous owners which give them a human touch. If someone has left a slip with notes about some aspect of the contents within the pages, don't throw it out.
5. Consider small privately printed books about textile subjects as a way of easily getting together a unique collection of books not normally found in stores. Some of these may be rather skimpy how-to booklets but many are on good stock, with lovely drawings and very personal touches not found in trade books. See Chapter 8 for a directory of several such books to get started.

OLD TEXTILE MAGAZINES

This is a subject particularly dear to my heart. Any reader who has kept track of things I own will have realized that I am far from immune to the collecting bug. However, in most instances my collecting involves a few inherited things, and items bought here and there to add to what I had. My crochet hook collection is not much bigger than that of any crocheter who keeps a wardrobe of usable hooks at hand. It is in the area of old needlework magazines that I most nearly fall into the category of serious collector for ever since my very first "haul" about twelve years ago I've added with steadfastness and purpose—buying magazines in choice condition which I carefully store in an antique trunk; as well as torn, used, and cut-up ones which I use for reference, collages, framed decorations, etc. On occasion I will cut pages from the torn group which contain things other people collect (like Kewpie paper dolls and Campbell Soup Kid ads) and trade them for an issue of some particular favorite of mine, such as *The Modern*

The author with a sampling of her favorite old needlework-oriented magazines. A cutwork table runner made by her grandmother is compared with a pattern for a similar one published in the early twentieth century. The magazine to the right of the author is opened to a page of illustrations and instructions for making rolled silk flowers such as those made by Nancy Lipe for her Victorian costume accessories in Chapter 4.

Priscilla. I also like the bound, gilt-edged old *Godey's* and *Peterson's* magazines.

Some very serious collectors are much more specialized than I. A few collect only covers, or will refine their collection to include complete runs of a magazine, or at least complete runs for a particular year. The heavily needlework-slanted magazines of most interest to the purist collector are those which are best known—i.e., *Godey's, Peterson's, Ladies' Home Journal,* with *Ladies' World* and *Modern Priscilla* edging up in popularity in the past several years. There are lots of other good things worth looking for in the dollar or less category—pulp paper publications put out for farm wives, specialized booklets published by embroidery materials suppliers and, best of all, if you can find them, the premium booklets advertised in some of the above-mentioned publications.

Since many of the old magazines are in imperfect or less-than-choice condition, recyclers and doers will find them most usable for their contents, and for reference. The torn and cut-apart magazines can provide an excellent opportunity to turn paper memorabilia into fabric memorabilia. For example, if you like hankies with images of old illustrations, like May Stinger's hankie on page 46, you can with the aid of a product called Fabulon create your own old hankie if you have a magazine with similar pictures. With the aid of this specially coated paper, the magazine image can be transformed into an iron-on decal. The result would be an authentic paper-on-fabric item which might be described as mixed era. Fabulon is available in most hobby shops, or write to Sangray, P.O. Box 2388, Pueblo, Colo., 81004; att: Merry Janes.

CURRENT TEXTILE MAGAZINES

The increased interest in the various aspects of the fiber and fabric crafts was bound to bring into existence a whole new harvest of magazines. The increased price of publications makes saving every magazine subject to strong temptation but while magazine rates have gone up so has the cost of living space and most people simply cannot indefinitely save all the publications they enjoy in the course of a year. Weeding out the things you can't or don't want to store can be done in a way which will ensure their being collected rather than burnt in a trash pile. Check with textile-oriented organizations or textile and home economics departments of universities and see if they would like your periodical accumulations for their libraries. Many will jump for joy at your offer. A recent newsletter of C.H.A.N., the Center for the History of American Needlework, carried a pleased thank you to a California woman who had provided their library with a complete (1970–1977) run of *Ladies' Home Journal Needle and Craft.*

For your own private collection, my suggestion is to zero in on the best of the specialized textile magazines and newsletters which have been launched recently enough for you to obtain all issues without too much trouble. If these magazines continue publication, your complete run will increase in value and in interest since you can see the changes wrought by success. Some will go under for economic reasons or because of the independent nature of these publishers, which leads them in new directions. These too will increase in value as they become "former" publications. Either way *you* can't lose. Two examples of this kind of collecting would be a small newsletter for stitchery enthusiasts which was launched for a three-year run in June 1975 by Robbie Fanning of 632 Bay Road, Menlo Park, California, and *Fiber Arts*, a bimonthly newsletter which has grown into what promises to be an important textile magazine. See annotated resource chapter for details.

OTHER PAPER MEMORABILIA

Once a craft becomes sufficiently popular for someone to produce printed patterns for hobbyists to follow, thousands upon thousands of reproductions will be made. The Berlin patterns which produced a veritable flood of housewife-made needlework are a case in point; the patterns for rug hooking issued by Edward Sands Frost are another. Esthetically, the products resulting from this kit creativity are less interesting for a collector than originally designed work, though there are always exceptions where the kit design changes by virtue of the handcrafter's innovations. Rarer and probably more valuable than any of the end products are the original patterns.

The Center for the History of American Needlework has, through its unique approach to collecting, opened the door to all manner of ideas you might pursue as an individual. For example:

Slides, prints, and postcards picturing needlework and textiles or textile activity
Textile business cards
Advertising brochures and catalogues from needlework and textile suppliers
Advertising and editorial matter using needlework as part of the graphic design
Short stories that mention needlework
Exhibition catalogues
Letters, diaries, and other manuscript material by needleworkers, including manuscript patterns and sketches
Posters and announcements of textile publications

Rachel Maines, the director of C.H.A.N., has pretty much sublimated her own collecting into the Center's work though she admits

she still has a passion for textile machinery prints, especially machinery predating 1930. "You can't imagine what a conversation piece a print of a Davis and Furrier teasel gin makes in your living room . . . or a mule spinner," she confides.

Having saved but not collected some of the above-mentioned memorabilia, I know that all of the suggestions are valid ones. Some fiber artists' business cards are indeed small gems of art. The idea of collecting short stories mentioning needlework rang a very personal chord since I've not only kept my own list of such stories already written but often toyed with the idea of writing a thriller centered around a textile gallery. A number of characters in the book would be strangled—as it turns out by threads woven into the hanging tapestries so that the mystery's solution literally hangs by a thread! I have also taken to clipping articles and book references which contain textile language and since beginning this book have even discovered a best-selling novel with a heroine who is a curator at the Cloisters, "a Ph.D. in art history, with the beginning of a good collection of Sumerian fragments" (*The Girl That He Marries*, Rhoda Lerman).

7.
Things Every Textile
Collector Should Know

By now you are familiar with the highways and byways open to you as a traveler along the textile collecting trail. To round out your know-how let us consider how you can buy what you like at the prices which will be most to your liking, and how you can best care for and maintain those things for which you have successfully bargained. Finally, while a book like this cannot really teach you how to actually do textile crafts, I shall detail the basic methods employed for some of the recycled collectibles scattered throughout these pages.

Bargaining and Buying Tips and Pitfalls

Everybody loves a bargain, but not everybody likes to bargain, or knows how to do it right. They're either too timid, or too outrageous in their methods. The timid might shore up their courage to haggle a bit with the realization that many a dealer will actually find acquiescence to the first price asked since such unquestioning assent may forever leave her wondering if she asked for enough.

For the overly shrewd, Roald Dahl's priceless story, "Parson's Pleasure" (*Kiss, Kiss,* 1953, Alfred A. Knopf, Inc., and also a Dell paperback) should serve as a vivid reminder anytime they are inclined to outfox themselves by pushing their bargaining luck. The parson of the Dahl story is actually a London antiques dealer who has hit upon a way of finding and buying farmhouse treasures by pretending to collect old furniture for the Society of the Preservation of Rare Furniture. When the "parson" chances upon a rare Chippendale breakfront he is not content to enjoy his find at the farm owner's price, but gets caught up in the bargaining ruse of belittling the piece in order to further reduce the cost. "It's only the legs that have any interest at all," he complains to the farmer and his sons. When at last they agree to his terms and he goes off to fetch his van, the farmers take him at his word and cut off the legs to save him the trouble of hauling off the "worthless" and heavy remains!

If there is a key to striking a sensible, honorable, and successful bargain, it can be found somewhere between timidity and/or super-fastidiousness and the "parson's" tasteless and reprehensible temerity.

A bargaining transaction at its simplest would go something like this: The buyer, upon seeing something he or she likes, inquires, "How much is that _____?" The dealer will respond in a fairly disinterested manner, unlike the regular store clerk who tends to come forward, anxious to be of help the minute a spark of interest is shown. The antique store owner tends to conserve energy until your attitude seems properly serious. It is this seeming disinterest and near unfriendliness that intimidates the nonbargainer from asking the next question, "Would you sell it for less?" From here things become crucial. "What do you want to pay?" is a typical dealer response which puts the ball back into your lap. Should you name an outrageously low price, in preparation for a lengthy bit of haggling, or should you ask for something in the nature of a ten percent discount? Your decision depends upon your intuitiveness about the other person, your ability to assess general prices in this particular location, the rarity of the object, how badly you want it at this moment, and how much money you have.

If your judgment is sound, your first offer will be accepted and the bargain can be concluded with goodwill on both sides. To cite a specific example: In Chapter 2 you will see a photograph of a jacket made from a less-than-perfect knitted bedspread bought at a Wyoming farm sale for $3. Shortly after seeing this jacket I stopped at a shop on a New York State highway. Among the knitted, crocheted, and lace oddments, there was a bedspread almost identical in style and condition. Eastern dealers, even off the highway, unlike those out West, have been aware of the new uses to which many people are putting old handwork and their prices reflect this. Things are sold by the piece rather than in more advantageous-to-the-buyer box lots so that while prices may still be affordable, the 50¢ and $1 or more per item add up. I was not surprised to have the dealer quote $8. Using Bucky King's $3 spread as my guideline for making a counteroffer, I felt reasonably sure that the $5 discount needed to match the $3 purchase would be turned down. In this case paying twice as much in New York than Wyoming would still mean a chance to buy a well-made and fairly inexpensive item. A $2 discount would more than likely be palatable to the dealer, and so it was. It was in the same store that I bought the machine-made lace illustrated on page 79. The asking price was $3 and since under $5 taking off half rather than a quarter often works, I offered $1.50 for the "package." The bargain was instantly sealed.

Modest as these just-described transactions were they more or less typify bargaining. There are of course variations to the dialogue depending upon what and where you buy. In an open market, especially in a foreign country, bargaining is considered more of a game, a way of having a conversation with strangers. In Africa, for example, the first price is considered the "joking price" and if the tourist is willing to play his role in the "conversation" there is a whole set of actions and interactions such as laughing, throwing up hands on the seller's part—turning away on the buyer's part—that precede the final sale.

There are price-fixed situations everywhere even in countries known for their receptivity to bargaining. Furthermore, many antique buyers mistakenly think that when they buy handcrafted things in a gallery or directly from a craftsperson at a fair or studio, that bargaining here is also the expected thing. While some young, beginning artists will, especially at fairs, offer to give a special price, there is a difference between buying from a person who owns but did not make an object and from the maker who has invested his or her own personal energies. If you can't afford what a craftsperson has to offer, ask if there is anything within your means and, if not, take the craftsperson's card and save it for a time when you feel more flush.

Don't rule out bargaining if you buy old things by mail. All it takes is an extra letter with a counteroffer, and the basis for your offer should be pretty much the same as when you deal face-to-face. Someone recently offered me eight issues of an out-of-print magazine at $4 each plus postage. I counteroffered with $20 postpaid and received a happy letter of acceptance.

To conclude, here are some buying and bargaining do's and don'ts:

1. Bargain privately, when you and the seller are out of earshot of customers, preferably by yourselves.

2. Don't act as if you hate something. If you weren't interested you wouldn't be inquiring about the price, and the seller knows this as well as you. Conversely, don't show off about how you're going to use your purchase. In short, show your interest, but hide your passion—and talents, if you're a recycler.

3. If you're buying expensive items, a cash discount is considered a legitimate bargaining point—just as deposits and time payments are far from unusual!

4. Carrying price guides is poor psychology. Besides, most of these are not too accurate.

5. Take your cue from dealers who buy by the box and sell by the piece. If things are not boxed but scattered around a room or

table, point them out and ask "how much for the whole lot?" Remember though that nothing is a bargain unless you need or love it so don't buy quantity solely for the sake of the price.

6. If you prefer to do your buying close to home, take advantage of the bargaining advantages accruing to the "regular" customer. Once you frequent a shop and buy things, no matter how modestly, the shop owner will regard you as a friend and may be more inclined to give you a good deal. Special bargains might come your way by means of a little judicious trading either of information or merchandise. If you buy something elsewhere which you feel the shop owner would like, you might offer to sell it to her at the price for which you bought it, in exchange for some other bargain, or perhaps as a swap.

7. When in a foreign country, don't make an offer on the first thing you see. The further from the main arrival spots you go, the better the quality and prices.

8. Attending auction previews has already been mentioned and cannot be stressed enough. The earlier you get there the better. Watch the pros, listen to the questions. Write down the price you want to pay during the inspection and *stick to it*. Inform yourself about terms and rules and be clear as to the units which comprise a bid.

Knowing and Caring for Your Treasures

The same urge for neatness and order which seems to replenish the stocks of resale shops also accounts for a great deal of destructive tampering with things best left untouched by cleaning solutions, soap, water, or high-speed vacuums. Many a gray hair on a textile curator's head may be attributed to housewives who have applied the old adage about cleanliness being next to Godliness to inherited and otherwise acquired textile items.

You need not master the science of textile conservation, and a science it is, to own textiles; but, since there are plenty of people who have this mastery why not benefit from their experience and advice *before* you remove an old sampler from its frame or scrub away at a spot on a carpet or fabric, or give an old quilt the "gentle" suds treatment touted by detergent manufacturers.

A number of museums have days set aside for the public to bring in textiles in order to help them know more about the provenance of what they have as well as how to deal with cleaning, remounting, and storage. For example, in the nation's capital alone there are two such resources: at the Smithsonian Institution's Museum of History and Technology, textile curator Doris Bowman has set aside Friday as "bring in" day, while the Textile Museum offers a similar service on the first Saturday of every month. Don't overlook your state's agricultural extension service either. This division of the Department of

Agriculture often employs people who have been trained in general textile knowledge. Yet another excellent source for help and information is the environmental design and/or fiber department of a university. Some design and art conservation teachers in these departments act as private consultants. One such expert, Michael Bogle, formerly of Syracuse University's School of Environmental Design, and currently curator at the Merrimac Valley Textile Museum, offers the following specifics for identifying and cleaning fabrics:

1. The kind of care given to textiles should be determined by the material itself. A silk crepe could shrink 50 percent in a water cleaning, while washing gently with water could improve lots of cottons.

2. If you choose to wash things without enlisting professional advice and help, proceed with caution. Test *every* color first with the intended cleaning solution. Avoid even the mildest detergents except for items known to be washable and colorfast (i.e., crocheted cotton doilies, antimacassars, etc.) since most detergents contain undesirable brighteners.

3. For the actual cleaning, avoid scrubbing and abrasion. Use only very small amounts of detergent to ease rinsing. Thorough rinsing is very important.

4. Let the item dry flat if possible since textiles, especially woolens and silks, are often weaker when wet. (Author's Note: I personally like soft terry towels as drying "boards.") Suspending the textile in netting during the cleaning allows it to be moved and dried in the same netting. Using a hair dryer for small items hurries things up, though Professor Bogle does not feel valuables should be rushed.

5. Since irons can spit out rust or other terrible muck without warning, never use a steam iron. Professor Bogle considers simple pressing on some flat surface best, though a warm iron, especially when applied over fabric sandwiched between towels, is endorsed by many.

6. Dry cleaning should be done by a professional, preferably not the neighborhood dry cleaner. This is a health as well as a safety precaution since fumes and solvents in a small home space can be extremely dangerous.

7. Oriental carpets are not only expensive to buy but to clean, with costs ranging from 70¢ to $3 a square foot. Michael Bogle admits to using his driveway for an occasional application of the experts' long-known alternative method of cleaning: Beat the rug and then lay it face down for about six hours on *fresh* snow. All the dirt will get pulled into the cold snow.

8. Fabrics can be identified by burning small samples of fibers. Use a flame source that does not emit an odor, such as a candle. Take a few tufts of the fiber and move slowly toward the flame, observ-

ing the way the fiber reacts to the flame. Smell the odor produced (for nylons and polyesters this is often the only way to identify) and examine the residue. The following chart provided by Professor Bogle can be used as a guideline:

Fibers	*Odor*	*Residue*	*Support Flame?*
Cotton Linen Rayon	burning paper	gray, soft ash	yes, no melting
Acetate Triacetate	vinegar	dark bead, hard	yes, some melting
Wool Silk Chinon	singed hair	crumbling dark ash	no, does not melt
Nylon	celery-like	hard tan bead	occasionally, with considerable drip
Qiana	sweet, benzene	hard tan bead	less drip than nylon
Polyester	sweet, perfume-like	hard tan bead	occasionally, drips molten polymer
Acrylic	sharp, chemical	black bead	yes, no drip
Modacrylic	sharp, chemical	hard black bead	no, does not drip

REPAIRS, MOUNTING, DISPLAY, AND STORAGE

Some textiles you buy require attention to prevent additional or future deterioration of the fibers. Rips and worn spots in a rug, for example, should be fixed to avoid spreading. A latex backing can prevent a frayed rug from falling apart. Framed and mounted needlework is subject to the corroding effects of the acids in wood backings. This means that something like a sampler should be removed, cleaned, and remounted with clean muslin and an acid-free matting board between the original backing and the fabric. If you buy an old or new unframed sampler it should be mounted and framed with the same precautions in mind. A mail-order company which specializes in conservation supplies such as acid-free mounting paper, antitarnish tissues, and so forth is Talas (104 Fifth Avenue, New York, New York, 10011) though I would suggest you avail yourself of one of the aforementioned information resources before taking any action on your own.

Antique clothing should be cleaned and stored with the same special care given to nonwearable textiles. The silk blouses and dresses which have attracted so many thrift and antique shop buyers can be hand-laundered, but first be sure the fabrics won't run when wet (for example, very bright or printed silks). Once you've wet a piece snippped from an inside seam to see if it will hold its color, then you can wash it with pure soap flakes. The flakes require hot water to dissolve, so let your washing solution cool *before* putting the garment in. As with other textiles, do not scrub. Instead, swish the garment around, then rinse clear. Do *not* drip dry as you would a nylon shirt, but wring out excess moisture (again, gently) before hanging to dry. Better still, roll the garment in a towel or other clean cloth. Ironing, as previously stated, should be without steam, at a low setting, and with a protective cloth. Small accessory items like pincushions, silk flowers, and bags, are hard to vacuum, but you can blow off dust with a hair dryer.

As for storage, hang dresses on padded hangers. Protect with old sheets or other clean cloths rather than plastic bags, which draw moisture—an already-established enemy of all textiles. Accessories collected for use rather than for display can be further protected by storing them in covered boxes; otherwise, use the above-mentioned hair dryer treatment or shake out by hand.

Hanging fabrics need to be properly supported. Some museums back their tapestries with support strips stitched invisibly to the reverse side. More recently many collectors have discovered Velcro strips to be effective aids for mounting. For anything very valuable and large you might follow museum custom of giving hangings an occasional rest by rolling them on a tube. Rolling fabric on tubes is considered ideal for storage. If you must fold, keep the folds to a minimum and take the time to refold large things periodically to avoid deep creases.

The best home you can give textiles is one with an even temperature and a minimum of humidity. To store pieces during humid seasons, be sure they are clean, fold between sulphite-free paper, and sprinkle with moth crystals.

DAY-TO-DAY USE AND PRECAUTIONS

Some people keep their textiles, especially those which are old, stored away for fear that they will get too worn. They'll wear out anyway, and in fact are likely to get mildewed and permanently creased all locked up, so take them out and enjoy them!

Do *not* display textiles within range of direct sunlight. Most people know about the dangers of fading but remember our beaded bag collector Marilyn Green's warning about the sun's actually disintegrating beads.

A pad underneath a floor rug will prolong its life, as will periodic shifting of position and reversing if it's reversible.

Rugs and hangings can be and actually should be vacuumed regularly but keep the suction low and use the soft wall-cleaner rather than the rug attachment. Annual mothproofing and professional cleaning is a sound practice.

Baskets of natural materials can be washed but *not soaked*. A brush-on coating of mineral oil will avoid a basket's becoming brittle and will restore an old one. Fiber baskets can be vacuumed like hangings and rugs.

Recycling and Reproduction Skills

Reweaving damaged tapestries or costly rugs and other repair work connected with valuable antique objects is, as already suggested, best left in the hands of experts, or at least undertaken with expert guidance. Even for those interested in finding new functions for fiber and fabric objects, there are crafts artists who will incorporate your finds, or theirs, into hangings, apparel, etc. For some, however, being able to do at least some simple recycling on their own adds special meaning and pleasure to the search for things to buy, and as I have stated several times, this need not involve extensive needlecraft skills. Sewing, embroidery skills, and basic crochet stitches can take you a long way. Since you will be working with many old things to create your new look and function, the illustrations accompanying these very rudimentary instructions are reproduced from old needlework magazines. For more in-depth and advanced techniques there are many contemporary, well-illustrated books as well as courses for all levels of proficiency and interest.

THE VERSATILE BUTTONHOLE STITCH

In addition to the basic running and back stitch there are some one hundred embroidery stitches. The Coats and Clark Company has a booklet available for just 50¢ in most variety stores which illustrates all of them for anyone who wants to master a complete stitch vocabulary. For those interested in one really all-purpose stitch to join or decoratively edge pieces of fabric and to use decoratively on fabric surfaces, I heartily recommend the buttonhole stitch. If added as an edging to woven or crocheted or knitted fabrics, it can be worked close together or spaced out for a netted, lacelike effect. It can be used to connect two separate pieces of fabric and even independently as an alternative to crochet. When used in this way, the beginning of the stitching yarn or separate yarn is used as a base for looping the buttonhole stitches back and forth or in circles to create cupped forms. Stitches can even be increased and decreased to control the forms, and when worked in this manner, buttonhole stitching is known as knotless netting. The Ecuadorian baskets pictured on page 89 are an example of very tight looping or knotless netting, with sturdy materials.

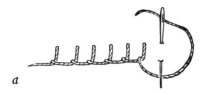

a

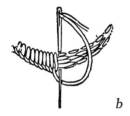

b

a. The buttonhole stitch worked as an edging for a handkerchief.
b. The buttonhole stitch tightly spaced and worked over a padding of stitches. Worked independently, as knotless netting, the base around which the looping is done would be an unattached piece of looping fiber.
c. Here we see the buttonhole stitch used to fill in cutwork in embroidery. The loops are worked all around the cut edges and toward the center. As the hole gets smaller, loops are skipped. This type of lace-like looping can also be done to join fabrics. The blouse made from sections of a crocheted tablecloth, page 11, used single crochet stitches to edge the cut segments, and buttonhole stitching or knotless netting to join the segments.

c

The uses of crochet to create original functional and art objects, to recycle existing crochet work or trim and decorate other types of fabrics is virtually limitless. Its prime advantage, like buttonhole stitching, is that it can be started from almost any kind of base and worked into many different shapes. For fabrics without holes into which to poke the crochet hook, start with a row of buttonhole stitches and then crochet into the buttonhole loops.

By making many stitches into the basic crochet stitch you can create ruffles. Skipping a stitch narrows the work. With some variations the single crochet stitch grows into a taller stitch, thus giving more leeway for shaping. To make circular and tubular shapes, the beginning and end of a basic chain are joined and the crocheting proceeds around and around, rather than back and forth.

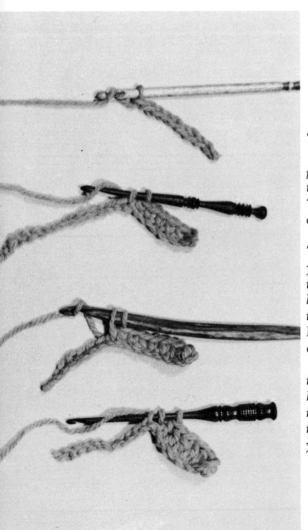

This illustration shows the variation in stitch sizes possible.

The top row shows the foundation chain being made. It is a process of placing a slip knot onto the crochet hook, bringing the yarn in front of this loop and pulling it through. This "yarning over" and pulling through the loop on the hook is continued until the foundation chain is the desired length.

In the second row, you see the basic single crochet stitch started. The hook is inserted into the chain of the foundation row. The yarn is brought in front as shown in the picture, and pulled through one of the two loops. The third row shows the stitch being completed, by bringing the yarn in front of the remaining two loops. This time it will be pulled through both loops. No matter what stitch you make, you will always have one loop on the hook when it is complete.

The bottom row illustrates a taller version of the basic stitch, the double crochet. The yarn is brought in front of the loop on the hook before inserting it into the base chain. The yarn is brought in front of the three loops as shown in the picture, and pulled through two of the three loops. To complete the stitch, bring the yarn in front again and pull through the remaining two stitches.

A flat piece of crochet is worked back and forth and in order to bring the stitches in alignment with each other from row to row, it is important to make an extra couple of chains *before* turning at the end of one row and beginning the next. When working in single crochet, make one extra chain. When working in double crochet, make two extra chains. The first stitch of the row is always made by inserting the hook into the chain next to the turning chain, which is actually the real first stitch of the row.

To end off a piece of crochet, cut the yarn to a six-inch length, pull through the loop and tighten.

To create an open space as in old-fashioned filet crochet, make a chain in between stitches. In short, crochet a stitch, make a chain and skip to the next stitch. By chaining up more than once and skipping more spaces, bigger holes will result.

To shape a piece from a wide to a narrow point, crochet two stitches together at the beginning of each row. To increase from a narrow to a wide point, go twice into the chain at the beginning of a row.

TWO CONTEMPORARY VICTORIAN RETICULES TO CROCHET

To test out the simplicity of the crochet basics just described, here are two little Victorian-style reticules with handles that give them

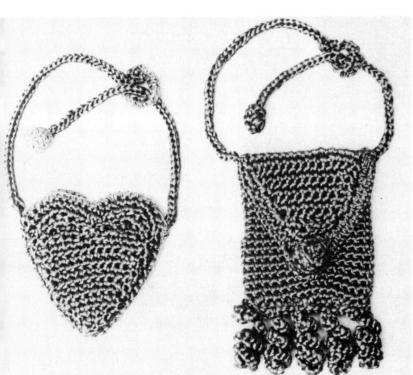

Two Victorian-style reticules in rattail designed for the beginning crocheter to make.

on-the-arm, over-the-arm, or over-the-shoulder wearability. The little stuffed balls used as closing and the ruffled additions on the envelope purse were favorites at one time not just for bags but for curtain and other trims. Shiny rattail in antique green or gold works well in carrying out the period flavor. A spool costing approximately $5.50 will be enough for both bags. Velour, ribbon or other novelty yarns could be substituted and many stores catering to weavers carry these types of supplies. I bought my rattail at Fibre Yarn, 840 Avenue of the Americas, New York, New York, 10001. While they are not a mail-order house per se, they will fill requests which are specific as to color and type of material.

To make the envelope bag: With a size E aluminum hook make a chain of 16 stitches. Crochet (single crochets throughout) back along the chain. When you get to the end of the row *do not turn*. Instead crochet around to the other side of the base chain and keep crocheting *around and around*. After a few rows you will have the beginnings of the envelope. Crochet for 20 rounds or whatever height you want for your bag. Work the lid by going *back and forth*, rather than in rounds. Decrease a stitch at the beginning of each row and end off when you reach a point.

Attach new yarn at one side of the lid and crochet until two stitches before the point. Make 4 chains, skip 4 chains, and crochet to the other side of the lid. Turn and crochet back for 1 row, this time crocheting the 4 raised chains and thus creating a closing loop.

To make the buttons for the closing, make a chain of 3 stitches and connect the first and last chain with a slip stitch. Crochet around and around, making 2 stitches into every chain for 2 rounds. Then crochet 2 rounds going just once into every stitch. Insert a bead or stuffing and reverse the procedure by crocheting 2 stitches together until the circle is closed. End off, leaving a long piece of yarn to sew the ball in place.

The strap is made in the manner of what Victorian ladies called watch chains. They made them on special U-shaped gadgets called lyres. You can use a toy-store knitting jenny or if you know how to knit, cast 3 or 4 stitches onto double-pointed needles and knit *without* ever turning the work, just pulling the yarn back to the beginning of each row.

The ruffles on the envelope bag are made by crocheting directly into the bottom with a chain of 12 to 15 stitches. On the return row, skip the first chain and then crochet 3 times into each stitch. You can make all the ruffles without breaking off the yarn; slip stitch from the end of one ruffle to the beginning of the next.

To make the heart bag: The heart bag is made of two identical pieces which are sewn, crocheted, or knotless-netted together. Start at the point by casting on 2 stitches and crochet back and forth, increasing a stitch at the beginning of each row until you have 14 stitches. To make the heart shape, make 2 single crochets, 3 double crochets, 2 single crochets—turn and make 3 single crochets, 2 doubles, 3 singles, and end off. Repeat this for the unworked 7 stitches and then make 1 row of single crochet stitches across the entire top.

The rest of the details are the same as for the other bag except that lamé yarns and a #2 crochet hook are used for the stuffed ball and lamé yarn is used to make a buttonhole-stitch border all around the bag.

8.
Annotated Resource Guide

Books to Expand Your Knowledge

As stated in Chapter 6 there are so many books published on the individual topics surveyed in this volume that buying within just one specialty could fill several shelves of a collector's library. Instead of listing a complete bibliography which would, without exaggeration, take up some twenty-five pages, I have chosen to list a sampling with annotations about contents.

CONSERVATION AND PRESERVATION

Finch, Karen, and Putnam, Greta. *Caring for Textiles*. New York: Watson-Guptill Publications, 1977.
 A slim but informative volume geared to the layman. Covers antique, exotic, and modern textiles. Illustrated.

Leene, J. E., ed. *Textile Conservation*. Washington, D.C.: Smithsonian Institution, 1972.
 More expert-oriented than the above.

Plenderleith, H. J. *The Conservation of Antiquities and Works of Art*. London: Oxford University Press, 1956.
 Written by the keeper of the British Museum, this is a scholarly text for museum conservators and covers all types of art works.

Talas Catalogue of Art Conservation Supplies. 104 Fifth Avenue, New York, NY 10001.

With catalogues more and more turning into "real" books, this seems appropriately placed here. Price $1.

DIRECTORIES

Contemporary Crafts Market Place. Compiled by the Research and Education Department of American Crafts Council; updated every other year. R. R. Bowker Company, New York.

Lists shops, galleries, fairs, shows, courses, organizations where contemporary crafts can be seen, bought, and learned. Available in reference departments of libraries or by mail from R. R. Bowker, Box 1807, Ann Arbor, MI 48106. Price $15.95.

Annotated Directory of Self-Published Textile Books. Sommertime Publications, P.O. Box E, Woodmere, NY 11598.

Self-published booklets rarely found through regular book outlets, with annotations about contents, authors, number of editions and brief background on this type of publishing. Copyright 1978. Price $1.50.

HGA Directory of Textile Collections in the U.S. Handweavers Guild of America, Inc., 65 LaSalle Road, West Hartford, CT 06107.

At $2.50, a best buy for anyone traveling through the U.S. and interested in visiting museums and historical societies with interesting textiles. Listings include information about nature of collection, special tours, docents, slides, booklets, gift items, hours, days.

For the international traveler, 50¢ and a note stating the country you plan to visit will get you a little packet of notes especially geared to textile buying and studying. Since recipients are asked to send inputs after a trip, travel notes are constantly updated.

Lubell, Cecil. *Textile Collections of the World*, Vols. 1 and 2. New York: Van Nostrand Reinhold Company, 1977.

Lavishly illustrated guide to textile collections, including details about whom to contact. Size and $30 pricetags make these volumes library references more than handy travel guides.

Museums of the World. New York: R. R. Bowker Company, 1973.

An international guide to all types of museums. Subject index has listings under costumes and textiles.

National Standards Council of American Embroiderers. *Directory of Where to Find Embroidery and Other Textile Treasures in the U.S.A.* Museum Information Services Committee, Box 45105, Tulsa, OK 74145.

Another handy organizational directory, similar to previously published HGA guide; price $2.50.

Andere, Mary. *Old Needlework Boxes and Tools. Their Story and How to Collect Them.* New York: Drake Publishers, Inc., 1971.

Both this and Sylvia Groves' book are excellent, well-illustrated documentation of textile tools and accessories.

Auld, Rhoda. *Molas.* New York: Van Nostrand Reinhold Company, 1977.

A good combination of history and how-to for mola lovers.

Baker, W. L. *The Silk Pictures of Thomas Stevens.* New York: Exposition Press, 1951.

For the Stevengraph collector.

Caulfield, Sophia Frances Anne, and Seward, Blanche C. *The Dictionary of Needlework: An Encyclopedia of Artistic, Plain, and Fancy Needlework.* Facsimile of 1882 edition. New York: Arno Press, Inc.

If you're looking for one inexpensive volume which combines historic information, illustrations for technique identification, and how-to, this 530-page volume with 800 illustrations is it.

Coleman, Dorothy S.; Coleman, Elizabeth A.; and Coleman, Evelyn J. *The Collector's Book of Dolls' Clothes in Miniature. 1700–1929.* New York: Crown Publishers, Inc., 1976.

As suggested in section on dolls, clothing offers a chance to collect clothing in miniature though not necessarily cheaply, as this book is not cheap. Written by an authority on doll collecting who has authored other doll manuals.

Contemporary Crafts Market Place. See listing under Directories—more than 40-page listing of fiber-related books.

Emery, Irene. *The Primary Structure of Fabrics.* Washington, D.C.: The Textile Museum, 1965.

Reference text for anyone interested in classification of fabric structures.

Encyclopedia of Textiles. The editors of *American Fabrics Magazine.* Englewood Cliffs, N.J.: Prentice-Hall, Inc., 1960.

For the serious book buyer, an informative and picture-filled reference.

Fiberworks. The Cleveland Museum of Art, 1977.

A catalogue of a major exhibition of contemporary fiber art. Beautifully illustrated with excellent introduction by Evelyn Svec Ward, herself an outstanding modern fiber artist.

Fox, Carl. *The Doll.* New York: New American Library, 1977.

Even if you're not a doll collector this $4.95 reproduction of the $35 edition is worth having. Nice pictures of rag and knitted dolls.

Franses, Jack. *European and Oriental Rugs for Pleasure and Investment.* New York: Arco Publishing Co., Inc., 1970.

If you can obtain this in its original $5.95 edition it will serve as well as some of the more lavish and lavishly priced books.

Gilbert, Maxwell. *Navajo Rugs.* Palm Desert, Calif.: Desert Southwest Publishing Company, 1963.

Rugs—past, present, future.

Groves, Sylvia. *The History of Needlework Tools and Accessories.* Hamlyn Pub. Group Ltd., England. Country Life Books, 42 Centre, Fletham, Middlesex, n.d.

A labor of love and very well done too. A good buy at its original $5.95 ticket if you can find.

Harbeson, Georgiana Brown. *American Needlework: The History of Decorative Stitchery and Embroidery from the Late 16th to the 20th Century.* New York, 1938. Reprint edition, Bonanza Books, 1 Park Avenue South, New York, NY 10016.

Most decorative textile historians agree that this continues to be the most comprehensive book on the subject of all facets of the decorative arts—quilts, coverlets, tools, accessories, and patterns are covered. A super buy at its $4.95 hardcover reprint price.

Johnson, Bruce. *A Child's Comforts.* New York: Harcourt Brace Jovanovich, Inc., 1975.

A book for the quilt collector whose special interest lies in quilts made for and by children.

Kapp, Kit S. *Mola Art from the San Blas Islands.* Cincinnati, Ohio: K. S. Kapp Publications, 1972.

Privately published paperback. Handy pocket reference for travelers.

Ketchum, William, Jr. *Hooked Rugs: A Historical and Collector's Guide, How to Make Your Own.* New York: Harcourt Brace Jovanivich, Inc., 1977.

Nice two-in-one history and how-to.

Kopp, Joel, and Kate. *American Hooked and Sewn Rugs, Folk Art Underfoot.* New York: E. P. Dutton & Co., Inc., 1975.

Well-written and illustrated by a collecting couple. A smaller, less expensive catalogue version of this is available from The Museum of American Folk Art, 49 West 53 Street, New York, NY 10019.

Larsen, Jack Lenor. *Beyond Craft: The Art Fabric.* New York: Van Nostrand Reinhold Company, 1973.

This is the book which the collector interested in contemporary wall hangings by living fiber artists will do well to study.

Liebetrau, Preben. *Oriental Rugs in Color.* New York: Macmillan, Inc., 1963.

History and pictorial guide to most commonly seen rugs and their traditions.

Lindquist, Myrtle. *Book of a Thousand Thimbles.* Des Moines: Wallace-Homestead Book Company, 1970.

Meilach, Dona Z. *A Modern Approach to Basketry with Fibers and Grasses.* New York: Crown Publishers, Inc., 1974.

As its title implies, this book invites consideration of the contemporary basket. Historic examples and how-to.

Miles, Charles, and Bovey, Pierre. *American Indian and Eskimo Basketry: A Key to Identification.* New York: Crown Publishers, Inc., 1959.

A plain, unglamorous, but very sound book especially for the collector.

Newman, Thelma R. *Quilting, Patchwork, Appliqué and Trapunto.* New York: Crown Publishers, Inc., 1974.

A well-priced interesting look at the new directions in quilting. How-to instruction included.

Pfannschmidt, Ernst-Erick. *Twentieth Century Lace.* New York: Charles Scribner's Sons, 1975.

An especially interesting book since it brings lacemaking and collecting into the present century.

Safford, Carleton L., and Bishop, Robert. *America's Quilts and Coverlets.* New York: E. P. Dutton & Co., Inc., 1971.

The number of quilt books and booklets published is mind-blowing. This is one of the biggest, most profusely illustrated of the last decade's issues. It encompasses all types of bed coverings, including coverlets. A less expensive paperback on Amish quilts only, by Bishop and Elizabeth Safanda, is also a good bet for collectors.

Sommer, Elyse, and Sommer, Mike. *A New Look at Crochet.* New York: Crown Publishers, Inc., 1975.

A survey of the craft's emergence from its doily past to contemporary innovations, showing examples from past and present, plus how-to. In this same series, on same note: *A New Look at Knitting, Wearable Crafts, A New Look at Felt.* Available from Sommertime Publications, P.O. Box E, Woodmere, NY 11598.

Teleki, Gloria Roth. *The Baskets of Rural America.* New York: Dutton Paperbacks, 1977.

A much-needed collector's guide.

Wilcox, R. Turner. *Dictionary of Costume.* New York: Charles Scribner's Sons, 1969.

In addition to this hardcover reference, there's a paperback reproduction of this author's earlier *The Mode in Costume.*

Wisczyk, Arlene Zerger, ed. *Treasury of Needlework Projects from Godey's Lady's Book.* New York: Arco Publishing Co., Inc., 1972.

Paperback facsimile to help collector, recycler, and reproducer. If you can find the originals, so much the better, of course.

Periodicals

ESPECIALLY FOR ANTIQUE LOVERS

The past decade has brought an influx of antiques publications in addition to those already established. Many are newspaper tabloids, some are beautiful glossy-stock magazines. None are geared to the fiber enthusiast per se, but all will contain ads and articles often enough to merit consideration.

Americana
American Heritage Publishing Co.
383 W. Center St.
Marion, OH 43202
  Slickly beautiful bimonthly. Coverage includes interesting sights and collectibles. Not terribly textile oriented. Subscription $12 a year, single copy $2.

American Antiques
RD 1, Box 241
New Hope, PA 18939
  Monthly, glossy-stock magazine geared to quality antiques. Lots of fine articles. Definitely interested in textiles—i.e., July 1977 issue, a special quilt issue worth collecting if you collect quilts. Subscription $10 a year, single copy $1.

(The) American Collector's Journal
P.O. Box 1431
Porterville, CA 93257
  Monthly tabloid, mostly classifieds. Subscription $5 a year.

Antique Gazette
929 Davidson Avenue
Nashville, TN 37205
  Another monthly tabloid. Slim but always seems to have something of interest. Subscription $4 a year.

Antiques and Arts Weekly
The Bee Publishing Co.
Newtown, CT 06470
  This is a favorite weekly tabloid with East Coast dealers and collectors who fondly refer to it as The Bee. Subscription $8 per year, single copy 20¢.

Antiques Journal
Box 1046
Dubuque, IA 52001
  Monthly, glossy-stock magazine, lots of articles, book reviews, news of shows, auctions, flea markets, "Ask Us" column. Subscription $7.95 a year, single copy $1.

Antiques Monthly
Box 2274
Birmingham, AL 35201
  Monthly tabloid geared to quality antique lover. Contributing editors well-known experts. Good reports on special and upcoming events. Also publishes an "inside dopester" type investment publication. $1 a copy.

(The) Antique Trader Weekly
Box 1050
Dubuque, IA 52001
This is a tabloid swap meet, loaded with classifieds. Textiles to be found under Miscellaneous. Subscription $11 a year.

The Collector
Drawer C
Kermit, TX 79745
Another tabloid monthly. A recent issue had a most intriguing piece on an old knitting machine identified by nine different readers. Subscription $7.50 a year, 75¢ a copy.

Early American Life
P.O. Box 1831
Harrisburg, PA 17105
Printed on "antique" stock and filled with interesting bits of Americana. Textiles are part of the whole, but only part, of course. Monthly. Subscription $8 a year, single copy $1.50.

Flea Market Quarterly
Box 243
Bend, OR 97701
With flea markets proliferating as they do, this can't possibly be a *complete* guide but since each issue contains a fill-in calendar for each of three months readers can round out information themselves. Subscription $6 a year, $2.25 a single issue.

Hobbies
1006 South Michigan Avenue
Chicago, IL 60605
This is the magazine in which Marilyn Green, one of our featured collectors, advertised for and found some great bag buys. Subscription $7 a year.

Maine Antique Digest
P.O. Box 358
Waldboro, ME 04572
Photo-rich tabloid. Primitive hooked rugs, dolls, bags, and samplers featured. Monthly except January. Subscription $9.50 a year.

(The) New York Antique Almanac
P.O. Box 135
Lawrence, NY 11559
Small monthly tabloid. Subscription $6 a year, 75¢ a copy.

SPECIAL-INTEREST MAGAZINES

Collector's Circle Gazette
150–11 14th Avenue
Whitestone, NY 11357
Quarterly newsletter of Collector's Circle, a thimble group. Subscription $1.

Craft Horizons
44 West 53 Street
New York, NY 10019
   This is the bimonthly magazine of the American Crafts Council. Information for and about contemporary crafts artists throughout the world. Reviews of shows and events. Announcements. April issue usually contains special insert detailing travel and study tours. Subscribing memberships $18, single issue $2.

Creative Crafts
Drawer 700
Newton, NJ 07860
   Bimonthly for crafts hobbyists; has column "Who's Who and What's What in Fibers" by Elyse Sommer. Subscription $6 a year, single copy $1.

Fiber Arts
3717 4th Street, N.W.
Albuquerque, NM 87107
   A newsletter which has grown into a very dynamic bimonthly magazine reporting on the contemporary fiber arts scene, with emphasis on the less traditional forms. Subscription $9 a year, single copy $1.50.

(The) Flying Needle
c/o Carol Thraikil, 12920 N.E. 32nd Place
Bellevue, WA 98005
   Quarterly journal of National Standards Council of American Embroiderers. Nice, slick, and informative publication. Subscription $10 with membership.

Interweave
2938 North County Road
Loveland, CO 80551
   Quarterly regional magazine for weavers. Subscription $6 a year, $1.50 a copy.

Lace Magazine
2141 West 29th Street
Long Beach, CA 90806
   A home-produced effort with reprints from old magazines. Subscription $5 a year, 75¢ a copy.

Needle Arts
Embroiderers' Guild of America, Inc.
6 East 45th Street
New York, NY 10017
   Quarterly. $12 Subscription part of membership in guild.

Needlepoint News
Box 668
Evanston, IL 60204
   A chatty, attractive bimonthly, easy to store and save for the collector. Subscription $7 a year, $1.45 a single issue.

Quarterly Journal
6 Queen's Square
London, W.C.IN 3 AR
   Great Britain's own textile crafts magazine. Subscription $5 a year.

Quilter's Journal
P.O. Box 270
Mill Valley, CA 94941
   Calendar and in-depth features. Subscription $5.50 a year, $1.25 an issue.

Quilter's Newsletter
Box 394
Wheat Ridge, CO 80033
   Monthly geared to contemporary quiltmaker. News of shows. Subscription $7 a year, 75¢ a copy.

(The) Rug Hooker, News and Views
W. Cushing & Co.
North Street
Kennebunkport, ME 04046
   Bimonthly publication with instructional articles. Subscription $7 a year.

Shuttle, Spindle and Dyepot
Handweavers Guild of America
65 LaSalle Road
West Hartford, CT 05107
   Quarterly. Technique, travel articles, book reviews, etc. Subscription $12.50 a year with membership.

Textile Museum Journal
Textile Museum
2320 South Street, N.W.
Washington, DC 20007
   Annual, with scholarly articles on textiles, book reviews, etc. Subscription $4.

Weaver's Newsletter
Box 259
Homer, NY 13077
   Features column "The Weaving Experience" by Elyse Sommer. Subscription $6 a year for 9 issues.

Working Craftsman
Box 42
Northbrook, IL 60062
   Quarterly devoted to all crafts but good fiber coverage, including a column "Fiber Lines" by collector-artist Bucky King. Subscription $9 a year.

Organizations

American Crafts Council
44 West 53 Street
New York, NY 10019

See Directories and Periodicals.
The Council also has available slide kits for purchase and rentals, many
on textiles. In its research library on the second floor, collectors can use
library of books and periodicals, as well as extensive juried biographical
and photo files of contemporary crafts artists. There is a large drawer for
fibers. Open only Tuesday, Wednesday, and Friday, 12 to 4 P.M.

Center for the History of American Needlework
Box 8162
Pittsburgh, PA 15217
$10 contribution brings an informal but informative quarterly newsletter,
discounts on reproductions of library materials, bibliography and other
reference listings, slides, and small exhibits (i.e., doily and potholder exhibits). Center is small, run by dedicated volunteers, and visitors to the
area are always welcome.

Crown Point Rugweavers' Assn.
Box 328
Crown Point, NM 87313
Indian weavers' association. Send stamped addressed envelope for calen-
dar of auction dates.

Embroiderers' Guild of America, Inc. (*See* Periodicals.)

Handweavers Guild of America
(*See* Directories and Periodicals.) This excellent organization has local
guilds which will put collectors in touch with fiber artists able to execute
commissions. Also has slide kits and a speakers' bureau.

International Old Lacers
Box 346
Att: Rachel Wareham
Ludlow, MA 01046
An organization started 24 years ago by four doll collectors who wanted
to know more about lace on dolls and which has grown to international
membership of more than 1000. Meetings and a bulletin.

National Quilting Association, Inc.
Margaret Todd, Box 62
Greenbelt, MD 20770
Quilters' organization with newsletters, for doers and collectors. Sub-
scriptions $5—$3 for senior citizens (hurrah!)

National Standards Council of American Embroiderers
(*See* Directories and Periodicals.)

Stevengraph Collectors Assn.
Att: Lewis Smith
Irvington-on-Hudson, NY 10533
    Members share information, bulletin $10 initiation.

Index